KU-649-036

BRAINSE SRAID
TEL: 6744888

Galway City People enjoying the nightlife at Quay St

lonely planet

GALWAY &
THE WEST
OF IRELAND

ROAD
TRIPS

Belinda Dixon

HOW TO USE THIS BOOK

Reviews

In the Destinations section:

All reviews are ordered in our authors' preference, starting with their most preferred option. Additionally:

Sights are arranged in the geographic order that we suggest you visit them and, within this order, by author preference.

Eating and Sleeping reviews are ordered by price range (budget, midrange, top end) and, within these ranges, by author preference.

Map Legend

Routes

▬▬▬ Trip Route
▬▬▬ Trip Detour
▬▬▬ Linked Trip
▬▬▬ Walk Route
─── Tollway
─── Freeway
─── Primary
─── Secondary
─── Tertiary
─── Lane
─── Unsealed Road
─── Plaza/Mall
▦▦▦ Steps
)═(Tunnel
▦▦▦ Pedestrian
      Overpass
─ ─ Walk Track/Path

Boundaries

─ ─ ─ International
─ ─ ─ State/Province
─── Cliff

Hydrography

~~ River/Creek
~~ Intermittent River
≈≈ Swamp/Mangrove
~~ Canal
    Water
    Dry/Salt/
    Intermittent Lake
    Glacier

Highway Markers

E44 E-Road Network
M100 National Network

Trips

1 Trip Numbers
9 Trip Stop
Walking tour
Trip Detour

Population

✪ Capital (National)
◉ Capital
   (State/Province)
● City/Large Town
○ Town/Village

Areas

Beach
Cemetery
  (Christian)
Cemetery (Other)
Park
Forest
Reservation
Urban Area
Sportsground

Transport

✈ Airport
⊕ Cable Car/
   Funicular
Ⓟ Parking
⊕ Train/Railway
⊕ Tram

Note: Not all symbols displayed above appear on the maps in this book

Symbols In This Book

☑ Top Tips   Food & Drink

🔗 Link Your Trips   Outdoors

💬 Tips from Locals   Essential Photo

↪ Trip Detour   Walking Tour

📖 History & Culture   Eating

👪 Family   Sleeping

- - - - - - - - - - - - - - - - - - - -

👁 Sights   🛏 Sleeping

🏖 Beaches   🍴 Eating

🏃 Activities   🍷 Drinking

🎓 Courses   ☆ Entertainment

👉 Tours   🛍 Shopping

🎉 Festivals & Events   ℹ Information & Transport

- - - - - - - - - - - - - - - - - - - -

These symbols and abbreviations give vital information for each listing:

📞 Telephone number
🕐 Opening hours
Ⓟ Parking
🚭 Nonsmoking
❄ Air-conditioning
@ Internet access
🛜 Wi-fi access
🏊 Swimming pool
🥗 Vegetarian selection
📖 English-language menu
👪 Family-friendly

🐾 Pet-friendly
🚌 Bus
⛴ Ferry
🚊 Tram
🚆 Train
apt apartments
d double rooms
dm dorm beds
q quad rooms
r rooms
s single rooms
ste suites
tr triple rooms
tw twin rooms

GABRIEL12/SHUTTERSTOCK ©

WELCOME TO
GALWAY &
THE WEST OF
IRELAND

Little wonder the west of Ireland is top of most must-see lists – apart from the weather, it has it all. Routes through Mayo offer wild, romantic beauty, without the crowds. Road tripping in timeless Connemara reveals one of Europe's most stunning corners, replete with intriguing villages, white beaches and tawny bogs.

Westport and Galway deliver pit stops full of fun and frolic, as do the music-filled bars of County Clare – all provide perfect soundtracks for the mesmerising landscapes of The Burren and the Aran Islands.

Leabharlanna Poiblí Chathair Baile Átha Cliath
Dublin City Public Libraries

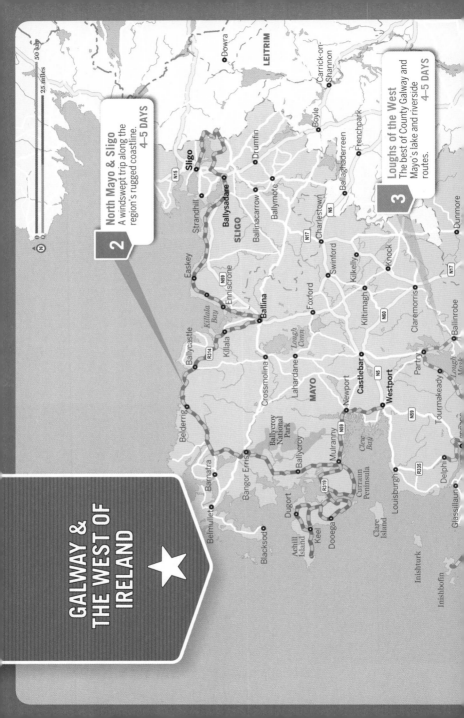

GALWAY & THE WEST OF IRELAND ★

2 North Mayo & Sligo
A windswept trip along the region's rugged coastline.
4–5 DAYS

3 Loughs of the West
The best of County Galway and Mayo's lake and riverside routes.
4–5 DAYS

0 — 50 km
0 — 25 miles

LEITRIM

Dowra
Carrick-on-Shannon
Boyle
Ballaghaderreen
Frenchpark
Dunmore

Sligo
N15
Strandhill
Easkey
Ballysadare
SLIGO
Drumfin
Ballinacarrow
Ballymote
Charlestown
N5
N17
Swinford
Kilkelly
Knock
Claremorris
N60
Kiltimagh
Ballinrobe
N17

Enniscrone
N59
Ballina
Foxford
Killala Bay
R314
Killala
Crossmolina
Lough Conn
Lahardane
MAYO
Castlebar
N5
Westport
N59
Partry
Lough Mask

Ballycastle
Belderrig
Barnatra
Belmullet
Bangor Erris
Ballycroy National Park
Ballycroy
Mulranny
Newport
Clew Bay
Curraun Peninsula
Louisburgh
Tourmakeady
Delph
Glassillaun
R335

Blacksod
Achill Island
Dugort
Keel
Dooega
R319
Clare Island
Inishturk
Inishbofin

N

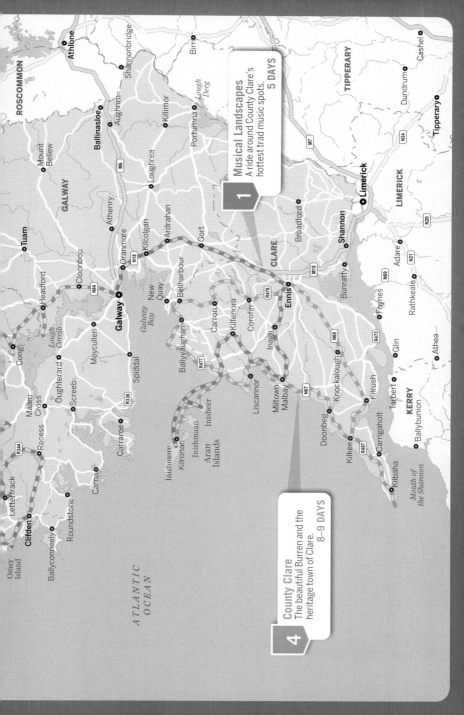

1

Musical Landscapes
A ride around County Clare's hottest trad music spots.
5 DAYS

4

County Clare
The beautiful Burren and the heritage town of Clare.
8–9 DAYS

GALWAY & THE WEST OF IRELAND

HIGHLIGHTS ★

DAWID K PHOTOGRAPHY/SHUTTERSTOCK ©

LUCA FABBIAN/SHUTTERSTOCK ©

Galway (left) Storied, sung-about and snug, Galway is one of Ireland's great pleasures. So much so that it's full of people who came, saw and still haven't brought themselves to leave. See it on Trips **1** and **3**

Connemara (above) A kaleidoscope of rusty bogs, lonely valleys and enticing hamlets laid across a patchwork of narrow country roads. See it on Trip **3**

Cliffs of Moher (right) The towering stone faces have a jaw-dropping, dramatic beauty that's enlivened by scores of sea birds, including cute puffins. See it on Trip **4**

OCSKAY BENCE/SHUTTERSTOCK ©

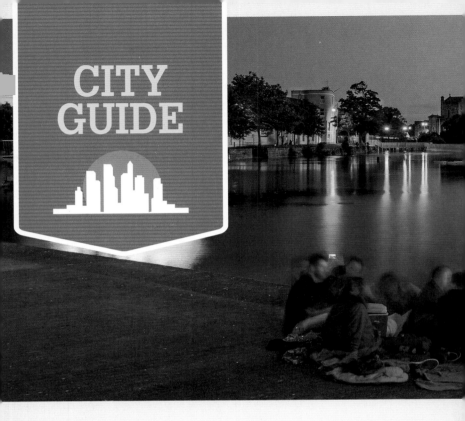

CITY GUIDE

GALWAY CITY

Ireland's most bohemian burg has long celebrated difference, which accounts for its vibrant arts scene, easygoing pace and outstanding nightlife. Old-fashioned pubs with traditional sessions, theatres hosting experimental works, designated music venues in thrall to the heartfelt outpourings of the singer-songwriter... It's just another night in Galway.

Getting Around

Traffic in and out of the city centre is a major issue during peak hours. The one-way system and network of pedestrianised streets can make getting around a little tricky.

Parking

Parking throughout Galway's streets is metered. There are several multistorey and pay-and-display car parks around town.

Where to Eat

Seafood is Galway's speciality, be it fish and chips, ocean-fresh chowder or salmon cooked to perfection. Galway Bay oysters star on many menus. Pedestrianised Quay St is lined with restaurants aimed at the tourist throngs.

RIHARDZZ / SHUTTERSTOCK ©

A Galway City evening during the Galway International Arts Festival

Where to Stay

Base yourself in the city centre so you can take full advantage of the city's tightly packed attractions. The west side, on the far side of the River Corrib, is where you'll find the best concentration of eateries, classic pubs and music venues.

Useful Websites

Discover Ireland (www.discoverireland.ie) Sights, accommodation bookings, discounts.

Galway Pub Guide (www.galwaycitypubguide.com) Comprehensive guide to the heaving scene.

Galway Tourism (www.galwaytourism.ie) Local tourist information.

Road Trips Through Galway:

Destination Coverage: p52

For more, check out our city and country guides. www.lonelyplanet.com

11

NEED <u>TO</u> KNOW

CURRENCY
Euro (€)

LANGUAGES
English, Irish

VISAS
Not required by most citizens of Europe, Australia, New Zealand, USA and Canada.

FUEL
Petrol (gas) stations are everywhere, but are limited on motorways. Expect to pay €1.35 per litre for unleaded (€1.25 for diesel).

RENTAL CARS
Avis (www.avis.ie)
Europcar (www.europcar.ie)
Hertz (www.hertz.ie)
Thrifty (www.thrifty.ie)

IMPORTANT NUMBERS
Country code (☏353)
Emergencies (☏999)
Roadside Assistance (☏1800 667 788)

Climate

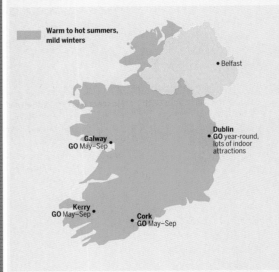

Warm to hot summers, mild winters

Belfast

Dublin
GO year-round, lots of indoor attractions

Galway
GO May–Sep

Kerry
GO May–Sep

Cork
GO May–Sep

When to Go

High Season (Jun–mid-Sep)
» Weather at its best.

» Accommodation rates at their highest (especially in August).

» Tourist peak in Dublin, Kerry and southern and western coasts.

Shoulder (Easter–May, mid-Sep–Oct)
» Weather often good: sun and rain in May, often-warm 'Indian summers' in September.

» Summer crowds and accommodation rates drop off.

Low Season (Nov–Easter)
» Reduced opening hours from October to Easter; some destinations close.

» Cold and wet weather throughout the country; fog can reduce visibility.

» Big city attractions operate as normal.

Your Daily Budget

Budget: Less than €60
» Dorm bed: €12–20

» Cheap meal in cafe or pub: €6–12

» Pint: €4.50–5 (more in cities)

Midrange: €60–150
» Double room in hotel or B&B: €80–180

» Main course in midrange restaurant: €12–25

» Car rental (per day): €25-45

Top End: More than €150
» Four-star hotel stay: from €150

» Three-course meal in good restaurant: around €50

» Top round of golf from €90

Eating

Restaurants From cheap cafes to Michelin-starred feasts, covering every imaginable cuisine.

Cafes Good for all-day breakfasts, sandwiches and basic dishes.

Pubs Pub grub ranges from toasted sandwiches to carefully crafted dishes.

Hotels All hotel restaurants take nonguests. A popular option in the countryside.

Eating price indicators represent the cost of a main dish:

Eating Costs
€ less than €12

€€ €12–25

€€€ more than €25

Sleeping

Hotels From chain hotels with comfortable digs to Norman castles with rainfall shower rooms and wi-fi.

B&Bs From a bedroom in a private home to a luxurious Georgian townhouse.

Hostels Every major town and city has a selection of hostels, with clean dorms and wi-fi. Some have laundry and kitchen.

Sleeping price indicators represent the cost of a double room in high season:

Sleeping Costs
€ less than €80

€€ €80–180

€€€ more than €180

Arriving in Ireland

Dublin Airport
Rental cars Rental agencies have offices at the airport.

Taxis Taxis take 30 to 45 minutes and cost €25 to €30.

Buses Private coaches run every 10 to 15 minutes to the city centre (€6).

Cork Airport
Rental cars There are car-hire desks for all the main companies.

Taxis A taxi to/from town costs €22 to €26.

Bus Every half hour between 6am and 10pm to the train station and bus station (€2.80).

Dun Laoghaire Ferry Port
Train DART (suburban rail) takes about 25 minutes to the centre of Dublin.

Bus Public bus takes around 45 minutes to the centre of Dublin.

Mobile Phones

All European and Australasian phones work in Ireland, as do North American phones not locked to a local network. Check with your provider. Prepaid SIM cards cost from €10.

Internet Access

Wi-fi and 3G/4G networks are making internet cafes largely redundant. Most accommodation places have free wi-fi, or a daily charge (up to €10).

Money

ATMs are widely available. Credit and debit cards can be used in most places, but check first.

Tipping

Not obligatory, but 10% to 15% in restaurants; €1/£1 per bag for hotel porters.

Useful Websites

Entertainment Ireland (www.entertainment.ie) Countrywide listings.

Failte Ireland (www.discoverireland.ie) Official tourist-board website for the Republic.

Lonely Planet (www.lonelyplanet.com/ireland, www.lonelyplanet.com/ireland/northern-ireland) Destination information, hotel bookings, traveller forum and more.

For more, see Road Trip Essentials (p108).

Road Trips

O'Brien's Tower, Cliffs of Moher (p100)
JOHANNES RIGG / SHUTTERSTOCK ©

Musical Landscapes

From the busker-packed streets of Galway city, this rip-roaring ride guides you around County Clare and the Aran Islands to delight in fine festivals and traditional-music pubs.

1

TRIP HIGHLIGHTS

155 km

Inisheer
End-of-the-earth landscape and traditional drumming festival

START
Galway

Inishmore

9
FINISH

Doolin ● Lisdoonvarna
Kilfenora

4

Miltown Malbay

2

65 km

Ennistimon
Country village with roaring Cascades and music at every turn

Ennis
Medieval town simply bursting with trad sessions and fine pubs

110 km

5 DAYS
155KM / 96 MILES

GREAT FOR...

BEST TIME TO GO
The summer months for outdoor *céilidh* (traditional music and dancing) and music festivals.

 ESSENTIAL PHOTO
Set-dancing at the crossroads, in Vaughan's of Kilfenora.

 BEST FOR TUNES
Ennis, on summer nights, where local musicians showcase their skills.

1 Musical Landscapes

Prepare for an embarrassment of musical riches. Join the big bawdy get-togethers of Galway's always-on music scene and Ennis' rollicking urban boozers. Then take a seat at the atmospheric small pub sessions in crossroad villages like Kilfenora and Kilronan on the Aran Islands, where pretty much everyone joins in. Whatever way you like it, this region is undeniably one of Ireland's hottest for toe-tapping tunes.

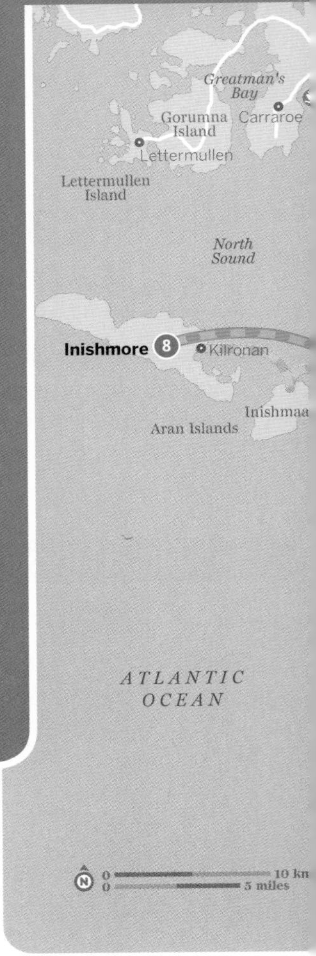

Greatman's Bay

Gorumna Island Carraroe
○ Lettermullen
Lettermullen Island

North Sound

Inishmore ⑧ ○ Kilronan

Inishmaa
Aran Islands

ATLANTIC OCEAN

Ⓝ 0 _____ 10 kn
   0 _____ 5 miles

❶ Galway City (p52)

Galway (Gaillimh) has a young student population and a largely creative community that give a palpable energy to the place. Walk its colourful medieval streets, packed with heritage shops, street-side cafes and pubs, all ensuring there's never a dull moment. Galway's pub selection is second to none and some swing to tunes every night of the week. **Crane Bar** (☎091-587 419; www.thecranebar.com; 2 Sea Rd;

⊙10.30am-11.30pm Mon-Thu, to 1am Fri, 12.30pm-1am Sat, to 11.30pm Sun), an atmospheric old pub west of the River Corrib, is the best spot in Galway to catch an informal *céilidh* most nights. Or for something more contemporary, **Róisín Dubh** (☎091-586 540; www.roisindubh.net; 9 Upper Dominick St; ⊙5pm-2am Sun-Thu, to 2.30am Fri & Sat) is *the* place to hear emerging international and local singer-songwriters.

The Drive » From Galway city centre, follow the coast road (R338) east out of town as far as the N18 and then cruise south to Ennis, where your great musical tour of Clare begins.

TRIP HIGHLIGHT

❷ Ennis (p92)

Ennis (Inis), a medieval town in origin, is packed with pubs featuring trad music. **Brogan's**

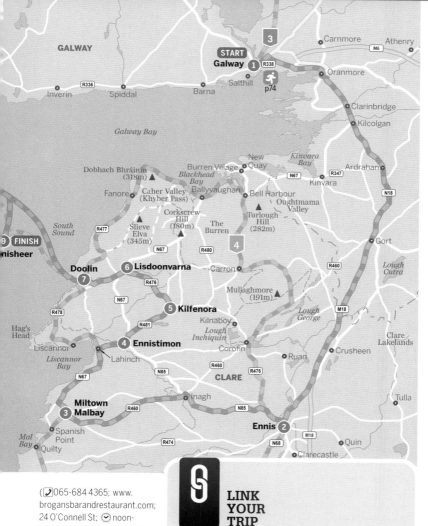

(📞065-684 4365; www.
brogansbarandrestaurant.com;
24 O'Connell St; 🕐noon-
midnight), on the corner
of Cook's Lane, sees a
fine bunch of musicians
rattling even the stone
floors almost every night
in summer, while the
wood-panelled **Poet's
Corner Bar** (📞065-682
8127; www.flynnhotels.com;

**LINK
YOUR
TRIP**

**3 Loughs of
the West**

Cruise Galway's
gorgeous inland
waterways on this tour of
its lakes and rivers.

**4 County
Clare**

Discover the beautiful
Burren and the heritage
towns of County Clare.

Old Ground Hotel, O'Connell St; ⏰11am-11.30pm Mon-Thu, to 12.30am Fri & Sat, noon-11pm Sun; 🛜) is a hideout for local musicians serious about their trad sessions. The tourist office collates weekly live music listings for the town's pubs. **Cois na hAbhna** (☎065-682 4276; www.coisnahabhna.ie; Gort Rd; ⏰opening hours vary), a pilgrimage point for traditional music and culture, has frequent performances and a full range of classes in dance and music; it's also an archive and library of Irish traditional music, song, dance and folklore. Traditional music aficionados might like to time a visit with **Fleadh Nua** (www.fleadhnua.com; ⏰May), a lively festival held in late May.

The Drive » From the N85, which runs south of The Burren, you'll arrive at the blink-and-you'll-miss-it village of Inagh. Swing right on to the smaller R460 for the run into Miltown Malbay – some 32km in all.

3 Miltown Malbay (p98)

Miltown Malbay was a resort favoured by well-to-do Victorians, though the beach itself is 2km southwest at **Spanish Point**. To the north of the Point there are beautiful **walks** amid the low cliffs, coves and isolated beaches. A classically friendly place in the chatty Irish way, Miltown Malbay hosts the annual Willie Clancy Summer School, one of Ireland's great trad music events. In town, one of a couple of genuine old-style places with occasional trad sessions is **Friel's Bar** (Lynch's; ☎065-708 5883; Mullagh Rd; ⏰6pm-midnight Mon-Thu, to 1am Fri & Sat, 2pm-midnight Sun) – don't be confused by the much bigger sign on the front proclaiming 'Lynch's'. Another top music pub is the dapper **Hillery's** (☎065-708 4188; Main St; ⏰3pm-1am).

ROBIN BUSH / GETTY IMAGES ©

The Drive » Hugging the coast, continue north on the N67 until you come to the small seaside resort of Lahinch. Just a few streets backing a wide beach, it's renowned for surfing. From here, it's only 4km up the road to the lovely heritage town of Ennistimon.

TRIP HIGHLIGHT

4 Ennistimon (p99)

Ennistimon (Inis Díomáin) is one of those charming market towns where people go about their business barely noticing the characterful buildings lining Main St. Behind this bustling facade there's a surprise: the roaring **Cascades**,

THE PIED PIPER

Half the population of Miltown Malbay seems to be part of the annual **Willie Clancy Summer School** (☎065-708 4148; www.scoilsamhraidhwillieclancy.com; ⏰Jul), a tribute to a native son and one of Ireland's greatest pipers. The eight-day **festival**, now in its fourth decade, begins on the first Saturday in July, when impromptu sessions occur day and night, the pubs are packed and Guinness is consumed by the barrel – up to 10,000 enthusiasts from around the globe turn up for the event. Specialist workshops and classes underpin the event; don't be surprised to attend a recital with 40 noted fiddlers.

Kilfenora Cathedral, County Clare

the stepped falls of the River Inagh. After heavy rain they surge, beer-brown and foaming, and you risk getting drenched on windy days in the flying drizzle. Not to be missed, **Eugene's** (☎065-707 1777; Main St; ⏰10.30am-11.30pm Mon-Thu, to 12.30am Fri & Sat, 12.30-11pm Sun) is intimate and cosy, and has a trademark collection of visiting cards covering its walls, alongside photographs of famous writers and musicians. The inspiring collection of whiskey (Irish) and whisky (Scottish) will have you smoothly debating their relative

merits. Another great trad pub is **Cooley's House** (☎065-707 1712; Main St; ⏰10.30am-11.30pm Mon-Thu, to 12.30am Fri & Sat, noon-11pm Sun), with music most nights in summer and several evenings a week in winter.

**The Drive ›› ** Heading north through a patchwork of green fields and stony walls on the R481, you'll land at the tiny village of Kilfenora, some 9km later. Despite its diminutive size, the pulse of Clare's music scene beats strongly in this area.

- - - - - - - - - - - - - - - - - -

❺ Kilfenora (p106)

Underappreciated Kilfe-nora (Cill Fhionnúrach)

lies on the southern fringe of The Burren. It's a small place, with a diminutive 12th-century **cathedral** (off Main St; ⏰9.30am-5.30pm Jun-Aug, 10am-5pm Mar-May, Sep & Oct), which is best known for its **high crosses**. The town has a strong music tradition that rivals that of Doolin but without the crowds. The celebrated **Kilfenora Céili Band** (www.kilfenoraceiliband. com) has been playing for more than a century. Its traditional music features fiddles, banjos, squeeze boxes and more and can be enjoyed most Wednesday evenings at

**WHY THIS IS A
CLASSIC TRIP**
BELINDA DIXON,
WRITER

To witness a proper traditional
session in one of the music houses
of Clare or the fine old pubs of
Galway can be a transcendent
experience, especially if it's
appropriately lubricated with a pint
(or few) of stout. Sure, there'll be
plenty of tourists about, but this is
authentic, traditional Ireland at its
most evocative.

Above: Traditional music session, Galway City
Left: Inisheer (p24), County Galway
Right: Eugene's pub (p21), Ennistimon, County Clare

MARIA JANUS / SHUTTERSTOCK ©

Linnane's Pub (☎065-708 8157; Main St; ◷10.30am-11.30pm, hours can vary). A short stroll away, **Vaughan's** (☎065-708 8004; www.vaughanspub.ie; Main St; ◷10.30am-11.30pm, hours can vary) has music in the bar every night during the summer and terrific set-dancing sessions in the neighbouring barn on Sunday nights.

The Drive » From Kilfenora the R476 meanders northwest 8km to Lisdoonvarna, home of the international matchmaking festival. Posh during Victorian times, the town is a little less classy today, but friendly, good-looking and far less overrun than Doolin.

- - - - - - - - - - - - - - - - -

❻ Lisdoonvarna (p105)

Lisdoonvarna (Lios Dún Bhearna), often just called 'Lisdoon', is well known for its mineral springs. For centuries people have been visiting the local spa to swallow its waters. Down by the river at **Roadside Tavern** (☎065-707 4084; www.roadsidetavern.ie; Kincora Rd; ◷noon-11.30pm Mon-Thu, to 12.30am Fri & Sat, to 11pm Sun Mar-Oct, shorter hours Nov-Feb), third-generation owner Peter Curtin knows every story worth telling. There are trad sessions nightly in summer and on Friday and Saturday evenings in winter. Look for a trail beside the pub that runs 400m down to two **wells** by the river. A few paces from the tavern, the **Burren Smokehouse** (☎065-707 4432; www.burrensmokehouse.ie; Kincora Rd; ⏰9am-6pm May-Aug, 10am-4pm Sep-Apr) is where you can learn about the ancient Irish art of oak-smoking salmon.

The Drive » Just under 10 minutes' drive west, via the R478/479, you'll reach the epicentre of Clare's trad music scene, Doolin. Also known for its setting – 6km north of the Cliffs of Moher – Doolin is really three small neighbouring villages. First comes Roadford, then 1km west sits Doolin itself, then another 1km west comes pretty Fisherstreet, nearest the water.

---

❼ Doolin (p102)

Doolin gets plenty of press as a centre of Irish traditional music, owing to a trio of pubs that have sessions through the year. **McGann's** (☎065-707 4133; www.mcgannspubdoolin.com; Roadford; ⏰10am-11.30pm Mon-Wed, to 12.30am Thu-Sat, to 11pm Sun; 🛜) has all the classic touches of a full-on Irish music pub; the action often spills out on to the street. Right on the water, **Gus O'Connor's** (☎065-707 4168; www.gusoconnorsdoolin.com; Fisherstreet; ⏰9am-midnight Mon-Thu, to 2am Fri-Sun), a sprawling favourite, has a rollicking atmosphere. It easily gets the most crowded and

has the highest tourist quotient. **McDermott's** (MacDiarmada's; ☎065-707 4328; www.mcdermottspub.com; Roadford; ⏰10am-11pm Sun-Wed, to 12.30am Thu-Sat) is a simple and sometimes rowdy old pub popular with locals.

The Drive » This 'drive' is really a sail – you'll need to leave your car at one of Doolin's many car parks to board the ferry to the Aran Islands.

---

❽ Inishmore (p64)

The Aran Islands sing their own siren song to thousands of travellers each year, who find their desolate beauty beguiling. The largest and most accessible Aran, Inishmore (Inis Mór), is home to ancient fort **Dun Aengus** (Dún Aonghasa; ☎099-61008; www.heritageireland.ie; adult/child €5/3; ⏰9.30am-6pm Apr-Oct, to 4pm Nov-Mar), one of the oldest archaeological remains in Ireland, as well as some lively pubs and restaurants in the only town, Kilronan. Irish remains the local tongue, but most locals speak English with visitors. **Tí Joe Watty's Bar** (☎086 049 4509; www.joewattys.ie; Kilronan; ⏰noon-midnight Sun-Thu, 11.30am-12.30am Fri & Sat Apr-Oct, 4pm-midnight Mon-Fri, noon-midnight Sat & Sun Nov-Mar) is the best pub in Kilronan, with traditional sessions most

summer nights. Turf fires warm the air on the 50 weeks a year when this is needed. Informal music sessions, glowing fires and a broad terrace with harbour views make **Tí Joe Mac's** (Kilronan; ⏰11am-11pm Mon-Thu, 11am-12.30am Fri & Sat, noon-10pm Sun; 🛜) another local favourite, as is the **Bar** (☎099-61130; www.inismorbar.com; Kilronan; ⏰noon-11pm Sun-Thu, 11.30am-midnight Fri & Sat), which has nightly live music from May to mid-October, and weekends the rest of the year.

The Drive » In the summer passenger ferries run regularly between the Aran Islands. They cost €10 to €15; schedules can be a little complex – book in advance.

TRIP HIGHLIGHT

❾ Inisheer (p69)

On Inisheer (Inis Oírr), the smallest of the Aran Islands, the breathtakingly beautiful end-of-the-earth landscape adds to the island's distinctly mystical aura. Steeped in mythology, traditional rituals are very much respected here. Locals still carry out a pilgrimage with potential healing powers, known as the *Turas,* to the Well of Enda, an ever-burbling spring in the southwest. For a week in late June the island reverberates to the thunder of traditional

HELIOSCRIBE / SHUTTERSTOCK ©

Gus O'Connor's pub, Doolin, County Clare

drums during **Craiceann Inis Oírr International Bodhrán Summer School** (www.craiceann. com; ☺late Jun). Bodhrán masterclasses, workshops and pub sessions are held, as well as Irish dancing. Rory Conneely's atmospheric inn **Tigh Ruairí** (Rory's; ☎099-75002; d €55-94; 🛜) hosts live music sessions and, here since 1897, **Tigh Ned** (☎099-75004; www. tighned.com; dishes €7-15; ☺kitchen noon-4pm Apr-Oct, bar 10am-11.30pm Apr-Oct) is a welcoming, unpretentious place, with harbour views and lively traditional music.

North Mayo & Sligo

2

Travel from country-cosmopolitan Westport to nature at its most visceral on windswept Achill Island. Then, carry on via superb surfscapes to Sligo, Yeats' beloved adopted home town.

TRIP HIGHLIGHTS

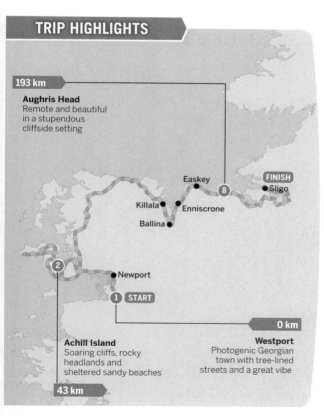

193 km

Aughris Head
Remote and beautiful in a stupendous cliffside setting

Easkey

FINISH
Sligo

8

Killala
Enniscrone

Ballina

2

Newport

1 **START**

0 km

Achill Island
Soaring cliffs, rocky headlands and sheltered sandy beaches

Westport
Photogenic Georgian town with tree-lined streets and a great vibe

43 km

4–5 DAYS
266KM / 165 MILES

GREAT FOR...

BEST TIME TO GO

In early autumn crowds have abated and the sea is warmest.

 ESSENTIAL PHOTO

Wild Atlantic rollers at sunset on Easkey beach.

 BEST FOR OUTDOORS

Achill Island and Easkey offer surf and blustery beach walks.

Achill Island The Blue Flag beach at Keem (p29)

2 North Mayo & Sligo

This area has something quietly special – the rugged and remote Atlantic scenery of the west, but with fewer crowds. Grab a board and face off an invigorating roller at Achill, take a restorative seaweed bath at Enniscrone, walk in WB Yeats' footsteps round the 'Lake Isle of Innisfree' at the foot of Benbulben and enjoy the unpretentious company of lively Westport.

TRIP HIGHLIGHT

1 Westport (p78)

Bright and vibrant even in the depths of winter, Westport is a photogenic Georgian town with tree-lined streets, riverside walkways and a great vibe. With an excellent choice of accommodation and restaurants and pubs renowned for their music, it's an extremely popular spot, yet has never sold its soul to tourism. A couple of kilometres west on Clew Bay, the town's harbour, Westport Quay

is a picturesque spot for a sundowner.

Westport House

(☎098-27766; www.westport house.ie; Quay Rd; adult/child house only €14/7, house & pirate adventure park €25/20; ☺10am-6pm Jun-Aug, to 4pm Mar-May & Sep-Nov, hours vary Dec-Feb; 🚼), built in 1730 on the ruins of the 16th-century castle of Grace O'Malley (p30), is a charming Georgian mansion that retains much of its original contents and has some stunning period-styled rooms. The house is set in glorious gardens. Children will

love the **Pirate Adventure Park**, complete with a swinging pirate ship, a 'pirate's playground' and a rollercoaster-style flume ride through a water channel.

The Drive >> A wiggling 12km drive north of Westport is the picturesque 18th-century village of Newport. Then comes Mulranny village on a narrow isthmus overlooking the 365 islands of Clew Bay. Just before the main R319 to Achill Island take the scenic route left (signed Ocean Rd). Once on Achill, cut left again to pick up Atlantic Dr, signed Wild Atlantic Way.

- - - - - - - - - - - - - - - - - -

TRIP HIGHLIGHT

② Achill Island (p81)

Ireland's largest offshore island, Achill (An Caol), is connected to the mainland by a short bridge. Despite its accessibility, it has plenty of that far-flung-island feeling: soaring cliffs, rocky headlands, sheltered sandy beaches, broad expanses of blanket bog and rolling mountains.

Slievemore Deserted Village (☺dawn-dusk), at the foot of Slievemore Mountain, is a poignant reminder of the island's past hardships. In the mid-19th century, as the Potato Famine took hold, starvation forced the villagers to emigrate, or die. Except in the height of the holiday season, the Blue Flag beaches at **Dooega**, **Keem**, **Dugort** and **Golden Strand** are often pretty much deserted.

The Drive >> The superbly scenic R319 bounces past broad inlets and high hills back towards the mainland. At the junction with the N59, turn left towards Ballycroy National Park. You're now deep amid beautifully bleak boglands dotted with drystone walls and sheep. About 14km later follow signs for the Ballycroy National Park Visitor Centre, and its cafe, Ginger & Wild.

- - - - - - - - - - - - - - - - - -

③ Ballycroy National Park

Covering one of Europe's largest expanses of

LINK YOUR TRIP

1 Musical Landscapes

Join the trail in Galway through the spiritual home of traditional Irish music.

3 Loughs of the West

Turn it down a little for a tour of the west's serene lakelands, from Sligo on the N17.

blanket bog, **Ballycroy National Park** (☏098-49888; www.ballycroynation alpark.ie; off N59, Ballycroy; ⏰10am-5.30pm Mar-Oct) is a gorgeously scenic region, where the River Owenduff wends its way through intact bogs. The park is home to a diverse range of flora and fauna including peregrine falcons, corncrakes and whooper swans. A nature trail with interpretation panels leads from the visitor centre across the bog with great views to the surrounding mountains. If you wish to explore further, the challenging, 40km **Bangor Trail** crosses the park and leads to some of its most spectacular viewpoints.

The Drive » Ballycroy is 18km south of Bangor Erris on the N59. Continuing north from here on to the R314, you'll pass the magnificent Stone Age monument at Céide Fields before heading through Ballycastle and on to the historic town of Killala.

④ Killala (p85)

The town itself is pretty enough, but Killala is more famous for its namesake **bay** nearby, and for its role in the French invasion, when in 1798 more than 1000 French troops landed at Kilcummin in Killala Bay. It was hoped that their arrival would inspire the Irish peasantry to revolt against the English. The rebellion though was short-lived; the events are marked by signs at Killala Quay – follow signs to it from the centre of town.

Lackan Strand, just to the west, is a stunning expanse of golden sand. There's good surf here, but you'll need to bring your own equipment.

The Drive » Back on the R314, it's only 12km or so down to the provincial hub of Ballina, a busy market town.

MICHAEL GISMO / SHUTTERSTOCK ©

⑤ Ballina (p86)

Mayo's second-largest town, Ballina, is synonymous with salmon. If you're here during fishing season, you'll see droves of green-garbed waders, poles in hand, heading for the River Moy – one of the most prolific rivers in Europe for catching the scaly critters – which pumps right through the heart of town. You'll also spot salmon jumping in the Ridge (salmon pool), with otters and grey seals in pursuit.

One of the best outdoor parties in the country, the five day **Ballina Salmon Festival**

THE PIRATE QUEEN

The life of Grace O'Malley (Gráinne Ní Mháille or Granuaile; 1530–1603) reads like an unlikely work of adventure fiction. Twice widowed and twice imprisoned for acts of piracy, she was a fearsome presence in the troubled landscape of 16th-century Ireland, when traditional chieftains were locked in battle with the English for control of the country. Grace was ordered to London in 1593, whereupon Queen Elizabeth I granted her a pardon and offered her a title: she declined, saying she was already Queen of Connaught. Westport House (p29) now resides on the ruins of Grace's 16th-century castle.

Aughris Head

(www.ballinasalmonfestival.ie) takes place in mid-July.

The Drive » Taking the N59 northeast out of town towards Enniscrone, cut back up to the coast on to the small R297, which you'll meet just over 4km from Ballina.

- - - - - - - - - - - - - - - - -

⑥ Enniscrone

Enniscrone is famous for **Kilcullen's Seaweed Baths** (📞096-36238; www. kilcullenseaweedbaths.net; Cliff Rd; bath from €25; ⏰10am-9pm Jun-Aug, noon-8pm Mon-Fri, 10am-8pm Sat & Sun Sep-May, closed Tue & Wed Nov-Mar), an Edwardian bathhouse that is one of the best and most atmospheric in the country. A stunning beach known as the **Hollow** stretches for 5km. Surf lessons and board hire are available from Enniscrone-based **Seventh Wave Surf School** (📞087 971 6389; www.surfsligo.com; Enniscrone Beach; lessons adult/child from €30/25; ⏰Apr-Oct).

The Drive » Some 14km north you'll come to the little village of Easkey.

- - - - - - - - - - - - - - - - -

⑦ Easkey

Easkey seems blissfully unaware that it's one of Europe's best year-round surfing destinations. Pub conversations revolve around hurling and Gaelic football, and facilities are few. The beach is signed from the eastern edge of town. It's overlooked by a 19m-high 12th-century ruined castle tower, the remains of a formidable stronghold. The uppermost level is known as the Sailor's Bed.

The Drive » From Easkey, hug the winding coast road (R297) until you see signs for Aughris Head.

- - - - - - - - - - - - - - - - -

TRIP HIGHLIGHT

⑧ Aughris Head

An invigorating 5km walk traces the cliffs around remote Aughris Head, where dolphins and seals can often be seen swimming into the

IRELAND'S SEAWEED BATHS

Ireland's native spa therapy is the stuff of mermaid (or merman) fantasy. Part of Irish homeopathy for centuries, steaming your pores open then submerging yourself in a seaweed bath is said to help rheumatism and arthritis, thyroid imbalances, even hangovers. Certainly it leaves your skin feeling baby-soft: seaweed's silky oils contain a massive concentration of iodine, a key presence in most moisturising creams.

Seaweed baths are prevalent along the west coast but two places stand out. **Kilcullen's Seaweed Baths** (p31), set within a grand Edwardian structure in Enniscrone, is the most traditional and has buckets of character. It seems perfectly fitting to sit with your head exposed and your body ensconced in an individual cedar steam cabinet before plunging into one of the original gigantic porcelain baths filled with amber water and seaweed.

For an altogether more modern setting, try **Voya Seaweed Baths** (☎071-916 8686; www.voyaseaweedbaths.com; Shore Rd; bath from €28; ☉10am-8pm), which has a beachfront location.

If too much relaxation is barely enough, both establishments also offer the chance to indulge in various other seaweed treatments, including body wraps and massages.

bay. Birdwatchers should look out for kittiwakes, fulmars, guillemots, shags, storm petrels and curlews along the way. In a stupendous setting on the lovely beach by the cliff walk, the **Beach Bar** (☎071-917 6465; www.thebeachbarsligo.com; mains €12-25; ☉food served noon-8pm daily summer, Fri-Sun winter; 🛜)is tucked inside a 17th-century thatched cottage, with cracking traditional music sessions and superb seafood.

The Drive » From Aughris rejoin the N59 heading broadly east and on to the N4 towards Sligo until you see a sign for Dromahair (R287). Take this small, leafy road east, skirting the south of Lough Gill.

----

⑨ Lough Gill (p91)

The mirrorlike 'Lake of Brightness', Lough Gill is home to as many legends as fish. One that can be tested easily is the story that a silver bell from the abbey in Sligo was thrown into the lough and only those free from sin can hear it pealing. (We didn't hear it...)

Two magical swathes of woodland – **Hazelwood** and **Slish Wood** – have loop trails; from the latter, there are good views of Innisfree Island, subject of WB Yeats' poem 'The Lake Isle of Innisfree'. You can take a cruise on the lake from **Parke's Castle**.

The Drive » Having soaked up the atmosphere of Yeats' backyard, make your way a few kilometres north, via the R288 and R286, to the hub of Yeats country, Sligo town.

----

⑩ Sligo Town (p88)

Sligo town is in no hurry to shed its cultural traditions but it doesn't sell them out, either. Pedestrian streets lined with inviting shopfronts, stone bridges spanning the River Garavogue, and *céilidh* (sessions of traditional music and dancing) spilling from pubs contrast with contemporary art and glass towers rising from prominent corners of the compact town. A major draw of Sligo's **County Museum** (☎071-911 1679; www.sligoarts.ie; Stephen St; ☉9.30am-12.30pm Tue-Sat, plus 2-4.50pm Tue-Sat May-Sep) is the Yeats room, which features photographs, letters and newspaper cuttings connected with the poet WB Yeats, as well as drawings by his brother Jack B Yeats, one of Ireland's most important modern artists.

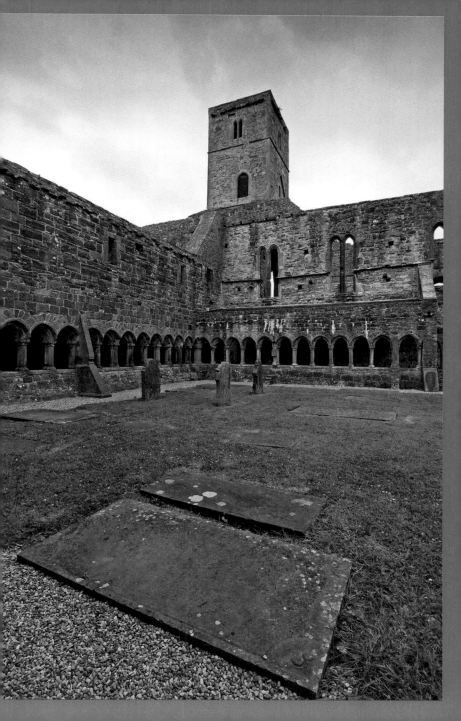

Loughs of the West

This trip takes you around beautiful, less-visited backwaters to see lakeside scenery at its most untarnished, visiting epic castles and intriguing islands en route.

3

TRIP HIGHLIGHTS

243 km

Inishbofin
Deserted lanes, green pastures and sandy beaches grace this sleepy island

128 km

Delphi
Striking mountains perfect for hiking or relaxing

(10) **FINISH**

Tourmakeady●
●Leenane
●Ballinrobe

(7)

(3)

58 km

Cong
Timeless Irish village immortalised by the classic film *The Quiet Man*

Galway●
START

4–5 DAYS
243KM / 151 MILES

GREAT FOR...

BEST TIME TO GO
May for ultimate fishing and the Inishbofin Arts Festival.

ESSENTIAL PHOTO
Cong, with the spectacular vista of Ashford Castle and the lake as backdrop.

BEST FOR FISHING
Loughs Corrib and Mask are world-renowned for their brown trout.

ough Corrib View from the village of Cong (p38)

35

3

Loughs of the West

Following the lay of the lakes, this panoramic waterside drive takes in the very best of Loughs Corrib and Mask. Pass the picture-postcard villages of Cong and Tourmakeady before crossing the barren beauty of Connemara to dramatic mountain-backed Delphi. Cruising Connemara's filigreed northern coast, you'll discover pretty strands and ancient remains both on the mainland and on the striking island retreat of Inishbofin.

Mt Knockmore (461m)

Inishturk

FINISH
⑩ **Inishbofin**   Renv
Poi
Inishshark

Cleggan

Omey ⑨ Claddaghd
Strand

Clifden

Ballinaboy

Ballyconneely

Slyne
Head   Ballyconne
Bay

*ATLANTIC
OCEAN*

---

❶ Galway City (p52)

Galway's Irish name, Gaillimh, originates from the Irish word *gaill,* meaning 'outsiders' or 'foreigners', and the term resonates throughout the city's history. Colourful and cosmopolitan – many dark-haired, olive-skinned Galwegians consider themselves descended from the Spanish Armada – this small city is best explored by strolling its medieval streets. Bridges arc the salmon-filled River Corrib, and a long promenade leads to the seaside suburb of **Salthill**, on Galway Bay, the source of the area's famous oysters. A favourite pastime for

Galwegians and visitors alike is walking along the seaside **Prom**, running from the edge of the city along Salthill. Local tradition dictates 'kicking the wall' across from the diving boards before turning around. In and around Salthill are plenty of cosy pubs from where you can watch storms roll over the bay.

The Drive » From Galway take the inspiringly named Headford Rd north on to the N84 into, well, Headford, skirting Lough Corrib, the Republic's biggest lake, which virtually cuts off western Galway from the rest of the country. At the crossroads in the centre of Headford turn left, initially following brown tourist signs for Rinnaknock Pier, then later for Greenfields.

---

❷ Lough Corrib

Just under 7km west of Headford, Greenfields pier juts out into Lough Corrib. Over 48km long and covering some 200 sq km, it encompasses more than 360 islands, including **Inchagoill**, home to some 5th-century

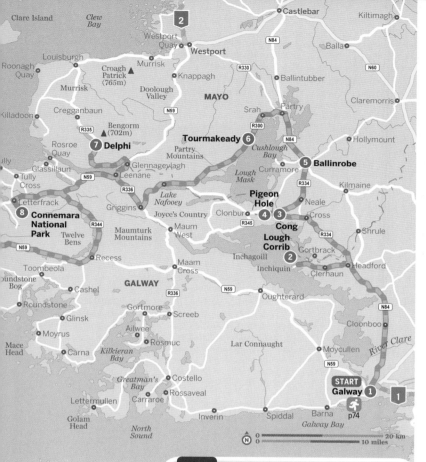

monastic remains, a simple graveyard and the **Lugnaedon Pillar** – a 6th-century inscribed stone. **Inchiquin** island can be accessed by a short, water-framed road from Greenfields pier. The lough is world-famous for its salmon and wild brown trout, with the highlight of the fishing

LINK YOUR TRIP

1 Musical Landscapes

This rip-roaring ride takes you from Galway's music bars to the best trad sessions of Clare.

2 North Mayo & Sligo

Continue exploring the northwest's incredible coastline, joining the route at Westport.

calendar being mayfly season, when zillions of the small bugs hatch over a few days (usually in May) and drive the fish – and anglers – into a frenzy. Salmon begin running around June. Upstream, signs point towards the curious **Ballycurrin Lighthouse**, built in 1772 when the lake may have seen more traffic – it's Europe's only inland lighthouse.

The Drive » From Headford, take the R334 north out of town as far as Cross, where you'll join the R346, which takes you into the outstanding village of Cong, some 16km later.

TRIP HIGHLIGHT

❸ Cong (p76)

Sitting on a sliver-thin isthmus between Lough Corrib and Lough Mask, Cong complies with romantic notions of a traditional Irish village. Time appears to have stood still ever since the evergreen American classic *The Quiet Man* was filmed here in 1951. Though popular on the

tour-bus circuit, the wooded trails between the lovely 12th-century **Augustinian abbey** (Mainistir Chonga; 094-954 6542; Abbey St; dawn-dusk) and stately **Ashford Castle** (094-954 6003; www.ashfordcastle.com; grounds adult/child €10/5; grounds 9am-dusk) offer genuine quietude. First built in 1228 as the seat of the de Burgo family, one-time owner Arthur Guinness (of stout fame) turned the castle into a regal hunting and fishing lodge, which it remains today. A range of **cruises** (www.corribcruises.com; adult/child €20/10) on Lough Corrib depart from the Ashford Castle pier.

The Drive » Next a 2km hop. From Cong take the R345 west out of town towards Cornamona. After you see the entrance for McGrath Quarry, take the first left then look out for the lay-by signed Pigeon Hole Wood.

❹ Pigeon Hole

Pick up the path leading left into the woods.

You're about to discover one of some half a dozen limestone caves that honeycomb the Cong area. Each has a colourful legend or story to its credit. **Pigeon Hole** is one of the best caves; steep, slippery, stone steps lead down towards it and subterranean water flows here in winter. Keep an eye out for the white trout of Cong, a mythical woman who turned into a fish to be with her drowned lover.

The Drive » After heading back into Cong, it's a 15-minute drive on the R345 and R334 north to Ballinrobe.

❺ Ballinrobe

The small market town of Ballinrobe (Baile an Roba), on the River Robe, is a good base for exploring trout-filled Lough Mask, the largest lake in the county. **St Mary's Church** has an impressive collection of stained-glass windows by Ireland's renowned 20th-century artist Harry

BOYCOTT BEGINNINGS

It was near the unassuming little village of Neale, near Cong, that the term 'boycott' first came into use. In 1880 the Irish Land League, in an effort to press for fair rents and improve the lot of workers, withdrew field hands from the estate of Lord Erne, who owned much of the land in the area. When Lord Erne's land agent, Captain Charles Cunningham Boycott, evicted the striking labourers, the surrounding community began a campaign to ostracise the agent. Not only did farmers refuse to work his land, people in the town refused to talk to him, provide services or sit next to him in church. The incident attracted attention from the London papers, and soon Boycott's name was synonymous with such organised, nonviolent protests. Within a few months, Boycott gave up and left Ireland.

MUSTANG_79 / GETTY IMAGES ©

Ashford Castle, Cong

Clarke. One depicts St Brendan 'the Navigator', with oar in hand, who reputedly sailed to America long before Columbus. You can access Lough Mask at **Cushlough Bay**, just 5km west of town. Take the Castlebar road north and immediately on the left you'll see signs for Cushlough. Follow these along winding lanes and eventually the road will open out into a wide car park with broad lough views. Here slender boats are pulled up on to the gravel and picnic tables dot the grass; it's a delightful place to pause and take in the views.

The Drive ›› Rejoin the N84 as it stretches north, before veering west at Partry. The landscape is made up of mostly small farm holdings, rusty bogland and tumbledown drystone walls. Follow the serene lakeside route (R300) before pit stopping to take in the lake around Tourmakeady.

- - - - - - - - - - - - - - - - - -

6 Tourmakeady

With the Partry Mountains acting as a picturesque backdrop to its west, the small village of Tourmakeady, on the shore of Lough Mask, is part of an Irish-speaking community. Once a flax-growing area, its name is derived from Tuar

Mhic Éadaigh, meaning 'Keady's field', referring to the field where the flax was once laid out to dry before spinning. Tourmakeady Woods, with a charming 58m-high **waterfall** at its centre, makes a wonderful spot for a picnic. Or head another 2km along R300 and refuel at the cosy **Paddy's Thatched Bar**, overlooking a shimmering expanse of water.

The Drive ›› Follow the swooping, curling lakeside road, pulling in at stunning Lake Nafooey, at the foot of Maumtrasna, to take in the view. Head north on the R336 through Leenane and around the

39

harbour, passing Assleagh Falls to Delphi, a scenic 45km in all.

- - - - - - - - - - - - - - - - -

TRIP HIGHLIGHT

❼ Delphi (p78)

Geographically just inside County Mayo, but administratively in County Galway, this swathe of mountainous moorland is miles from any significant population, allowing you to set about the serious business of relaxing. At the southern extent of the Doolough Valley, the area was named by its most famous resident, the second marquis of Sligo, who was convinced that it resembled the land around Delphi, Greece. If you can spot the resemblance, you've a better imagination than most, but in many ways it's even more striking than its Mediterranean namesake. At the beautiful Delphi Resort (p78) opt for a day's surfing, kayaking or rock climbing, followed by a stay and some pampering spa treatments.

The Drive » Return to Leenane and follow the N59 southwest to Letterfrack. Go through the town's crossroads and 400m later you'll see signs pointing left to the Connemara National Park Visitor Centre.

- - - - - - - - - - - - - - - - -

❽ Connemara National Park

Spanning 2000 dramatic hectares of bog, mountain and heath, Connemara National Park

encloses a number of the **Twelve Bens**, including Bencullagh, Benbrack and Benbaun. The heart of the park is **Gleann Mór** (Big Glen), through which the River Polladirk flows. There's fine walking up the glen and over the surrounding mountains. There are also short, self-guided walks and, if the Bens look too daunting, you can hike up **Diamond Hill** nearby. Various types of flora and fauna native to the area are explained, including the huge elephant hawkmoth, in the excellent **visitor centre** (📞076-100 2528; www.connemaranationalpark.ie; off N59, Letterfrack; 🕙9am-5.30pm Mar-Oct).

The Drive » Zip back east on the N59 for 9km before joining the R344 south through the Lough Inagh Valley as it skirts the brooding Twelve Bens. The N59 then sweeps west to Clifden. A few kilometres north signs point you towards Omey Island, a jagged coastal route that leads to tiny Claddaghduff (An Cladach Dubh).

- - - - - - - - - - - - - - - - -

❾ Omey Strand

Omey Island (population 20) is a low islet of rock, grass, sand and a handful of houses. Between half tide and low tide you can walk to the island (or if you're brave, drive) across the sand at Omey Strand. Tide times are displayed on the noticeboard in the car park; the route is marked by blue road signs bearing white arrows. Don't be tempted

to cross between half tide and high tide, or if there's water on the route.

The Drive » Return to Claddaghduff and head north to Cleggan to park and take the 30-minute ferry to Inishbofin.

- - - - - - - - - - - - - - - - -

TRIP HIGHLIGHT

❿ Inishbofin (p72)

By day sleepy Inishbofin is a haven of tranquillity. You can walk or bike its narrow, deserted lanes, green pastures and sandy beaches, with farm animals and seals for company. But with no *gardaí* (Irish Republic police) on the island to enforce closing times at the pub, by night – you guessed it – Inishbofin has wild craic. Situated 9km offshore, Inishbofin is only just under 6km long by 4km wide, and its highest point is a mere 86m above sea level. Inishbofin's pristine waters offer superb scuba diving, sandy beaches and alluring trails that encourage exploring. The island well and truly wakes up during the **Inishbofin Arts Festival** (www.inishbofin.com) in May, which includes accordion workshops, archaeological walks, art exhibitions and concerts. Ferries from Cleggan to Inishbofin are run by **Island Discovery** (📞095-45819; www.inishbofinislanddiscovery.com; adult/child return €20/10).

Inishbofin

JOHANNES RIGG/SHUTTERSTOCK ©

County Clare

Experience scenic coastline including the breathtaking Cliffs of Moher, the Aran Islands, market towns with cracking pubs and Clare's jewel, the geological wonder of The Burren.

4

TRIP HIGHLIGHTS

110 km

Inishmaan
Little-visited, breathtakingly beautiful and rich in mythology

④

Ballyvaughan

Cliffs of Moher

148 km ⑦

Ennistimon
An authentic market town with the Cascades at its centre

Ennis **START/ FINISH**

Kilrush

⑧

218 km

Loop Head
Spectacularly windswept and cliff-fringed

8–9 DAYS
299KM / 185 MILES

GREAT FOR...

BEST TIME TO GO

Spring for the awakening of nature in The Burren.

 ESSENTIAL PHOTO

A sunset shot over the Atlantic from Dun Aengus, Inishmore.

 BEST FOR RAMBLING

Take blustery cliff walks, or cross The Burren on foot.

Inishmore Cliffs of Dun Aengus (p64)

4 County Clare

From friendly market towns Ennis and Ennistimon down the cliff-fringed coast of Clare to its southernmost tip, the raggedly beautiful Loop Head, you'll encounter sandy strands and quiet coves just begging for company. In the summer you can island-hop between the Aran Islands, discovering historic relics and a taste of a simpler life, before returning to the mainland's homely resorts of Kilrush and Kilkee.

❶ Ennis (p92)

Ennis (Inis) is the busy commercial centre of Clare. It lies on the banks of the smallish River Fergus, which runs east, then south into the Shannon Estuary. It's the place to stay if you want a bit of urban flair; a little short on sights, Ennis' strengths are its food, lodging and traditional entertainment. The town's medieval origins are indicated by its irregular, narrow streets. Its most important

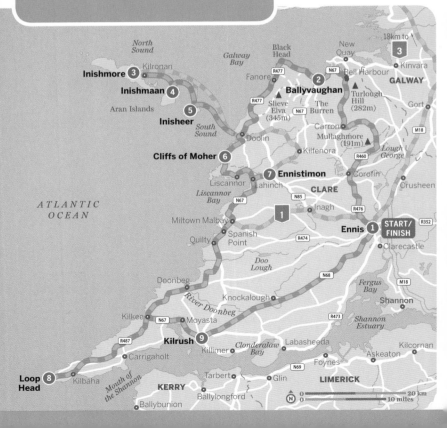

historical site is **Ennis Friary** (☎065-682 9100; www.heritageireland.ie; Abbey St; adult/child €5/3; ☺10am-6pm Easter-Sep, to 5pm Oct), founded in the 13th century by the O'Briens, kings of Thomond, who also built a castle here.

The Drive » A jaunt north, initially on the R476 towards Corofin, opens up the wondrous karst limestone of The Burren's heartland. Make sure you stop and take in primroses and other flora dotted in the crevices in spring. Skirting the Burren National Park, you'll turn left on to the N67 to get to Ballyvaughan. some 55km in all.

---

❷ Ballyvaughan (p107)

Something of a hub for the otherwise dispersed charms of The Burren, Ballyvaughan (Baile Uí Bheacháin) sits between the hard land of the hills and a quiet leafy corner of Galway Bay. Just west of the village's junction is

 LINK YOUR TRIP

 Musical Landscapes
Take a ride round County Clare's hottest trad music spots.

 Loughs of the West
Tour the best of County Galway and Mayo's lake and riverside routes.

the **quay**, built in 1829 at a time when boats traded with the Aran Islands and Galway, exporting grain and bacon and bringing in turf – a scarce commodity in the windswept rocks of The Burren.

The Drive » From Bally-vaughan the R477 clings to the coast, a leisurely 40-minute, shore-side ride down to Doolin, offering sweeping views over to the Aran Islands on your right. At Doolin, park and catch one of the ferries that run (between mid-March and October) to Inishmore, the first of three splendid castaway isles.

---

❸ Inishmore (p64)

Most visitors who venture out to the islands don't make it beyond 14km long Inishmore (Inis Mór) and its main attraction, Dun Aengus (p64), the stunning stone fort perched perilously on the island's towering cliffs. The arid landscape west of Kilronan (Cill Rónáin), Inishmore's main settlement, is dominated by stone walls, boulders, scattered buildings and the odd patch of deep-green grass and potato plants. It gets pretty crowded in summer but on foot or bike (for hire at the pier), you can happily set your own pace. There's an EU Blue Flag white-sand beach (awarded for cleanliness) at Kilmurvey, peacefully situated west of bustling

Kilronan. A **craft village** (Kilmurvey; ☺hours vary), where you'll find local women hand-knitting traditional Aran sweaters, sits nearby.

The Drive » Prebook your seasonal interisland boat ticket (€10 to €15) with one of the ferry companies and check their sailing schedules for the latest crossing times.

TRIP HIGHLIGHT

❹ Inishmaan (p67)

The least-visited of the islands, with the smallest population, Inishmaan (Inis Meáin) is a rocky respite. Early Christian monks seeking solitude were drawn to Inishmaan, as was the author JM Synge, who spent five summers here over a century ago. The island they knew largely survives today: stoic cows and placid sheep, impressive old forts and warm-hearted locals, who may tell you with a glint in their eye that they had a hard night on the whiskey the previous evening. Inishmaan's scenery is breathtaking, with a jagged coastline of startling cliffs, empty beaches, and fields where the main crop seems to be stone. **Teach Synge** (☎099-73036; €3; ☺by appointment Apr–mid-Sep), a thatched cottage on the road just before you head up to the fort, is where JM Synge spent his summers.

5 Inisheer (p69)

Inisheer (Inis Oírr), the smallest of the Aran Islands with a population of only around 200, has a palpable sense of enchantment, enhanced by the island's deep-rooted mythology, devotion to traditional culture and ethereal landscapes. Wandering the lanes with their ivy-covered stone walls and making discoveries here and there is the best way to experience the island. At **O'Brien's Castle** (Caisleán Uí Bhriain), a 100m climb to the island's highest point yields dramatic views over clover-covered fields to the beach and harbour. Much more modern is an iconic island sight – the freighter, **Plassy**, that was thrown up on the rocks in 1960 in a storm. An aerial shot of the wreck was used in the opening sequence of the seminal TV series *Father Ted*.

The Drive » Back on the mainland, it's back behind the wheel. From Doolin, it's a scenic 10-minute cruise on the coastal R478 to the famed, unmistakable Cliffs of Moher.

6 Cliffs of Moher (p100)

Star of a million tourist brochures, the Cliffs of Moher (Aillte an Mothair, or Ailltreacha Mothair) are one of Ireland's most visited sights. But, as at many over-crowded attractions, you have to get beyond the coach parties to experience what's drawn visitors in the first place – entirely vertical cliffs that rise to a height of 214m, with edges falling away abruptly into the constantly churning sea. A series of heads, the dark limestone seems to march in a rigid formation that amazes, no matter how many times you look. Luckily crowds thin the further you get from the coach park. And if you're willing to walk for 10 minutes south past the end of the 'Moher Wall', there's a trail along the cliffs to Hag's Head – few venture this far. A vast **visitor centre** (☎065-708 6141; www.cliffsofmoher.ie; R478; adult/child incl parking €8/ free; ☺8am-9pm May-Aug, to 7pm Mar, Apr, Sep & Oct, 9am-5pm Nov-Feb) is set back into the side of a hill, Hobbit house style. For uncommon views of the cliffs and wildlife you might consider a **cruise**. The boat operators in Doolin offer popular tours of the cliffs.

The Drive » A 10km drive through an ever-flattening landscape takes you to the small seaside resort of Lahinch. From there the N67 darts 4km due east to the authentic rural market town of Ennistimon.

TRIP HIGHLIGHT

7 Ennistimon (p99)

Ennistimon (Inis Díomáin; sometimes spelt Ennistymon) is a genuinely charming market town. Here a postcard-perfect main street is lined with brightly coloured shop-fronts and traditional pubs that host fantastic trad sessions throughout the year. From the roaring Cascades (p20), the stepped falls of the River Inagh, there are picturesque walks downstream. Each Saturday morning the stalls of a farmers market fill Market Sq.

The Drive » Next comes a 74km picturesque trip down the coastal N67 and then the R487. The landscape between the old-fashioned resort of Kilkee and Loop Head in the south has subtle undulations that suddenly end in dramatic cliffs falling off into the Atlantic. It's a windswept place with timeless striations of old stone walls.

TRIP HIGHLIGHT

8 Loop Head (p97)

Discriminating travellers are coming here for coastal views that are in many ways more dramatic than the Cliffs of Moher. On a clear day, Loop Head (Ceann Léime), Clare's southernmost point, has magnificent views south to the Dingle Peninsula crowned by Mt Brandon

Teach Synge cottage (p45), Inishmaan

AGE FOTOSTOCK / ALAMY STOCK PHOTO ©

GETTING TO & FROM THE ARAN ISLANDS

Flights and ferries serve the Aran Islands. Seasonal boats shuttle regularly from Doolin to the islands.

From mid-March to October, **Doolin 2 Aran Ferries** (☎065-707 5949; www.doolin2aranferries.com; Doolin Pier) and the **Doolin Ferry Co** (O'Brien Line; ☎065-707 5555; www.doolinferry.com; Doolin Pier) link the Arans with the mainland – they also run interisland services.

It takes around half an hour to cover the 8km from Doolin to Inisheer; a boat from the mainland to Inishmore takes at least 1¼ hours, while ferries from Doolin to Inishmaan take up to an hour. Expect to pay €20 to €25 return. Interisland boats cost €10 to €15. Each firm has an office at Doolin Pier or you can book online.

The ferry firms also offer various combo trips and Cliffs of Moher boat tours, which are best done late in the afternoon when the light is from the west.

Year-round, ferries also run to the Aran Island from Rossaveal, 37km west of Galway. **Aran Island Ferries** (☎091-568 903; www.aranislandferries.com; one-way/return €15/25) has two to three crossings daily; a shuttle bus is available from Galway city.

Aer Arann Islands (☎091-593 034; www.aerarannislands.ie; one-way/return €25/49) has flights to each of the islands up to six times a day; the journey takes about 10 minutes and can be done as a day trip. Flights go from **Connemara Regional Airport** (Aerfort Réigiúnach Chonamara; NNR; ☎091-593 034; Inverin); a shuttle bus links it with Galway city, 30km to the east.

(952m), and north to the Aran Islands and Galway Bay. There are bracing walks in the area including heritage trails around Kilkee and a 15km clifftop circuit. A working **lighthouse** (complete with fresnel lens) is the punctuation on the far southwestern point.

The Drive » A scenic 40km drive north on the R487 and east on the N67 brings you to the bustling local resort of Kilrush.

- - - - - - - - - - - - - - - - - -

🟢 Kilrush (p96)

Kilrush (Cill Rois) is a small, atmospheric town that overlooks the Shannon Estuary and the hills of Kerry to the south. From the town's big **marina**, you can head out on cruises run by **Dolphin Discovery** (☎065-905 1327; www.discoverdolphins.ie; Kilrush Marina; adult/child €26/14; ⊙late May–mid-Oct) to see the pods of bottlenose dolphins that live in the estuary, an important calving region for the mammals. The remarkable 'lost' **Vandeleur Walled Garden** (☎065-905 1760; www.vandeleurwalledgarden.ie; Killimer Rd; ⊙10am-5pm Tue-Sat) was the private domain of the wealthy Vandeleur family – merchants and landowners. The gardens are just east of the centre and have been redesigned and planted with colourful tropical and rare plants.

The Drive » After all that sea air and seafood you'll be ready for a straight 40-minute jaunt (on the N68) inland back to Ennis.

Colourful shopfront in Ennistimon (p46)

MARIA_JANUS/SHUTTERSTOCK ©

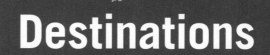

Destinations

County Galway (p52)
Ireland's liveliest city hums through the night, while some of Ireland's most picturesque scenery lies just outside the city limits.

Counties Mayo & Sligo (p76)
In these two counties you'll find all of Ireland's wild, romantic beauty but without the crowds.

County Clare (p92)
If the land is hard, Clare's soul certainly isn't: traditional Irish culture and music flourish here.

Street musicians performing in Galway City (p52)
JON CHICA/SHUTTERSTOCK ©

County Galway's exuberant namesake city is a swirl of colourful shop-lined streets, enticing old pubs, and an increasingly sophisticated food scene that celebrates local produce. And some of Ireland's most picturesque scenery fans out from Galway's city limits, from the breathtaking Connemara Peninsula to the wild and beautiful eroded swaths of the Aran Islands.

County Galway

GALWAY CITY

POP 79,934

Arty, bohemian Galway (Gaillimh) is one of Ireland's most engaging cities. Brightly painted pubs heave with live music, while restaurants and cafes offer front-row seats for observing buskers and street theatre. Remnants of the medieval town walls lie between shops selling handcrafted Claddagh rings, books and musical instruments.

While it's steeped in history, the city buzzes with a contemporary vibe, thanks in part to students, who make up around a fifth of the population. Its energy and creativity have seen it designated a European Capital of Culture for 2020.

History

From humble beginnings as the tiny fishing village Claddagh at the mouth of the River Corrib, Galway grew into an important town when the Anglo-Normans, under Richard de Burgo (also spelt de Burgh or Burke), captured territory from the local O'Flahertys in 1232. Its fortified walls were built from around 1270.

In 1396 Richard II granted a charter transferring power from the de Burgos to 14 merchant families or 'tribes' – hence Galway's enduring nickname: City of the Tribes. (Each of the city's roundabouts is named for one of the tribes.)

Galway maintained its independent status under the ruling merchant families, who were mostly loyal to the English Crown. Its coastal location encouraged a huge trade in wine, spices, fish and salt with Portugal and Spain. Its support of the Crown, however, led to its downfall; the city was besieged by Cromwell in 1651 and fell the following year. Trade with Spain declined and Galway stagnated for centuries.

The early 1900s saw Galway's revival as tourists returned to the city and student numbers grew. In 1934 the cobbled streets and thatched cabins of Claddagh were tarred and flattened to make way for modern, hygienic buildings, and construction has boomed since.

◉ Sights

★ **Galway City Museum** MUSEUM
(☏ 091-532 460; www.galwaycitymuseum.ie; Spanish Pde; ◷ 10am-5pm Tue-Sat, plus noon-5pm Sun Easter-Sep) FREE Exhibits at this modern, three-floor museum engagingly convey the city's archaeological, political,

cultural and social history. Look out for an iconic Galway hooker fishing boat, a collection of *currachs* (boats made of a framework of laths covered with tarred canvas) and sections covering Galway's role in the revolutionary events that shaped the Republic of Ireland.

★ Spanish Arch HISTORIC SITE
The Spanish Arch is thought to be an extension of Galway's medieval city walls, designed to protect ships moored at the nearby quay while they unloaded goods from Spain. It was partially destroyed by the tsunami that followed the 1755 Lisbon earthquake. Today it reverberates with buskers and drummers, and the lawns and riverside form a gathering place for locals and visitors on sunny days, as kayakers negotiate the tidal rapids of the River Corrib.

Galway Market MARKET
(www.galwaymarket.com; Church Lane; ⊙8am-6pm Sat, noon-6pm Sun) Galway's bohemian spirit comes alive at its street market, which has set up in this spot for centuries. Saturdays are the standout for food, when farmers sell fresh produce alongside stalls selling arts, crafts and ready-to-eat dishes. Additional markets take place from noon to 6pm on bank holidays, Fridays in July and August and every day during the Galway International Arts Festival (p55). Buskers add to the festive atmosphere.

Fishery Watchtower MUSEUM
(www.galwaycivictrust.ie; off Wolfe Tone Bridge; ⊙10am-4pm Tue-Fri, 11am-3pm Mon & Sat) FREE Constructed in the 1850s, this butter-coloured Victorian tower was used to monitor fish stock levels (and poachers). Now restored, the unique trilevel building contains a tiny museum that gives an overview of Galway's salmon-fishing industry through displays including photos, along with fantastic views over the waterways.

Galway Cathedral CHURCH
(Catholic Cathedral of Our Lady Assumed into Heaven & St Nicholas; ☑091-563 577; www.galway cathedral.ie; Gaol Rd; by donation; ⊙8.30am-6.30pm) Rising over the River Corrib, imposing Galway Cathedral is one of the city's finest buildings. Highlights include a beautifully decorated dome, attractive Romanesque arches, intricate mosaics and rough-hewn stonework emblazoned with copious stained glass. Regular musical events showcase the superb acoustics; look out for concerts, organ recitals, Gregorian chanting and Sunday morning Mass (11am), when the choir sings.

Hall of the Red Earl ARCHAEOLOGICAL SITE
(www.galwaycivictrust.ie; Druid Lane; ⊙9am-4.45pm Mon-Fri, 11am-3pm Sat) FREE In the 13th century, when the de Burgo family ruled Galway, Richard – the Red Earl – erected a large hall as a seat of power, where locals would arrive to curry favour. After the 14 tribes took over, the hall fell into ruin. It was lost until the 1990s, when expansion of the city's Custom House uncovered its foundations, along with more than 11,000 artefacts including clay pipes and gold cufflinks. The Custom House was built on stilts overhead, leaving the old foundations open.

Eyre Square PARK
Galway's central public square is busy in all but the harshest weather. A welcoming open green space with sculptures and pathways, its lawns are formally named Kennedy Park in commemoration of JFK's June 1963 visit to Galway, though locals always call it Eyre Sq. Guarding the upper side of the square is the **Browne Doorway**, an imposing, if forlorn, fragment from the home of one of the city's merchant rulers. Dating from 1627, it was relocated here from Abbeygate St in 1905.

Salthill Promenade WATERFRONT
See p36.

Tours

Galway Food Tours FOOD & DRINK
(☑086 733 2885; www.galwayfoodtours.com; 21 Shop St; €50; ⊙daily Wed-Sun) Galway's vibrant foodie scene shines through on these two-hour gourmet walking tours. Tastings include sushi, local cheeses, artisan breads and Galway Bay oysters. Booking is required. Tours leave from outside Griffin's Bakery.

Other tours include a six-hour pub trawl of Galway and Connemara, plus food-themed cycling and whiskey tours. All tours are also available in French.

Walking Tours of Medieval Galway WALKING
(☑091-564 946; www.galwaycivictrust.ie; ⊙2pm Tue & Thu May-Sep) FREE In the warmer months, the Dúchas na Gaillimhe (Galway

Galway City

COUNTY GALWAY GALWAY CITY

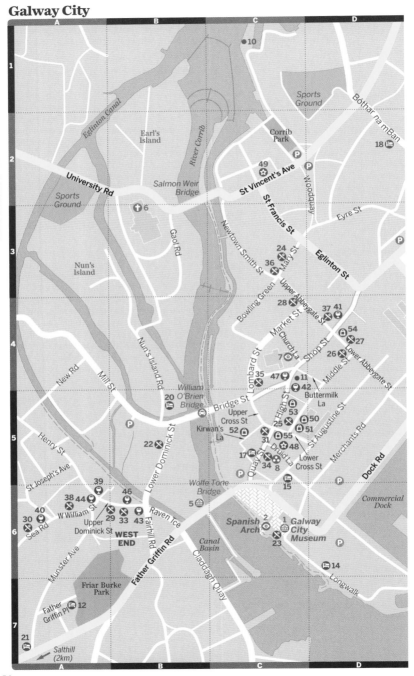

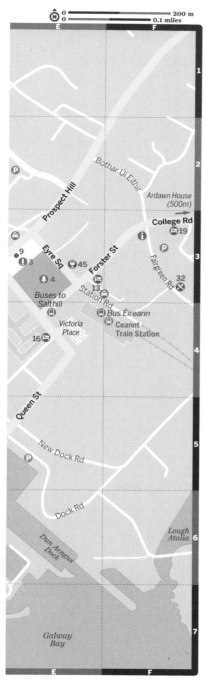

Civic Trust) runs free 90-minute guided walking tours of Galway's medieval centre. Tours depart from the Hall of the Red Earl (p53). Donations are welcomed.

City Sightseeing Galway BUS
(☎091-562 905; https://csgalway.palisis.com; Eyre Sq; 48hr tickets adult/child €12/7; ⊙10.30am-3pm Mar-Oct) Hop-on, hop-off open-top bus tours of the city and its environs set out from Eyre Sq. Buses run every 90 minutes and make 14 stops including Salthill. Two children travel free with every adult.

Corrib Princess CRUISE
(☎091-563 846; www.corribprincess.ie; Waterside, Woodquay; adult/child €17/8; ⊙May-Sep) Ninety-minute cruises aboard an open-top 157-seat boat pass castles and other historic landmarks along the River Corrib en route to the Republic's largest lake, Lough Corrib. In high season, there are two or three departures per day.

🎉 Festivals & Events

Galway Food Festival FOOD & DRINK
(www.galwayfoodfestival.com; ⊙Easter) The area's sublime food and drink are celebrated for five days over the Easter weekend with food and foraging tours, talks, cookery demonstrations and a market.

Cúirt International Festival of Literature LITERATURE
(www.cuirt.ie; ⊙Apr) Top-name authors converge on Galway over eight days in late April for one of Ireland's premier literary festivals, featuring poetry slams, theatrical performances and readings.

Galway Film Fleadh FILM
(www.galwayfilmfleadh.com; ⊙early Jul) Early July sees the six-day Galway Film Fleadh set screens alight with new, edgy works.

Galway International Arts Festival ART
(www.giaf.ie; ⊙mid-late Jul) Catch performances and exhibits by top drama groups, musicians and bands, comedians, artists and much more during this two-week fiesta of theatre, comedy, music and art.

Galway Race Week SPORTS
(www.galwayraces.com; ⊙late Jul-early Aug) Galway Race Week draws tens of thousands of punters for a week of partying. Races in Ballybrit, some 7km northeast of the city centre, are the centrepiece of Galway's most

Galway City

boisterous festival. Thursday's Ladies Day is a highlight, with best dressed and best hat competitions. Shuttle buses (return €9) link Galway city with the racecourse.

Galway Pride Festival LGBTQI+
(www.galwaypride.com; ⏱ mid-Aug) Started in 1989, Galway's Pride Festival (Ireland's first) runs for six days in mid-August and includes a flamboyant parade of floats through the city's streets. Dance, music, workshops, talks and family events also feature.

Galway International Oyster & Seafood Festival FOOD & DRINK
(www.galwayoysterfest.com; South Park; ⏱ late Sep) Going strong since 1954, the world's oldest oyster festival draws thousands of visitors. Events include the World Oyster Opening Championships, live music, a masquerade carnival and family activities.

Galway Christmas Market CHRISTMAS MARKET
(www.galwaytourism.ie; Eyre Sq; ⏱ mid-Nov–mid-Dec) Stalls selling traditional Christmas fare and gifts glow with candles and fairy lights during Galway's enchanting Christmas market.

🛏 Sleeping

Galway's festivals mean accommodation fills far in advance, particularly on weekends: book ahead.

B&Bs line the major approach roads (College Rd, a 15-minute walk from the centre, has an especially high concentration). To take full advantage of Galway's tightly packed attractions, though, try for a room in the centre itself.

Most B&Bs on College Rd have on-site parking but few central accommodation providers do, although many offer good deals at car parks.

★ Kinlay Hostel
HOSTEL €

(☑ 091-565 244; www.kinlaygalway.ie; Merchants Rd; dm/d/q €33/98/84; @ 🛜) The central location, cosy lounge, mellow vibe, pool table and smart kitchen and eating area make this large, brightly lit hostel a winner. Dorms vary in size but all the beds have individual curtains, lights and power and USB sockets. Tuesday night brings a pub crawl.

Snoozles Forster Street
HOSTEL €

(☑ 091-530 064; www.snoozleshostelgalway.ie; Forster St; dm €25-30, d €120; @ 🛜) Dorms (with four, six or 10 beds) and private rooms all have bathrooms at this sociable 130-bed hostel near the train and bus stations. Continental breakfast is free and facilities include a kitchen, barbecue terrace, pool table and lounge with piano, fiddles and guitars.

Sleepzone
HOSTEL €

(☑ 091-566 999; www.sleepzone.ie; Bóthar na mBan; dm €17-30, d/tr/q from €60/69/119; @ 🛜) In a bright red and yellow building, this big, busy backpacker base has over 200 beds in equally colourful dorms (most with their own bathrooms) and private rooms. Tea, coffee and toast are included. There's a large self-catering kitchen along with a coin-operated laundry and several lounges.

Galway City Hostel
HOSTEL €

(☑ 091-535 878; www.galwaycityhostel.com; Frenchville Lane, Eyre Sq; dm €33; @ 🛜) The awards keep rolling in for this cheery, orange-trimmed spot directly across from the train station, thanks to beds with electrical sockets and USB ports, privacy curtains in the bigger rooms, free continental breakfast, free printing, bike hire and a same-day laundry service. They'll also arrange tours, while live trad music plays in the downstairs bar.

★ Heron's Rest
B&B €€

(☑ 091-539 574; www.theheronsrest.com; 16A Longwalk; d €179-199; 🛜) The thoughtful hosts of this B&B in a lovely row of houses on the banks of the Corrib provide binoculars and deck chairs so you can sit outside and enjoy the views – views also extend from all

three snug but cute double-glazed rooms. Breakfasts incorporate organic local produce; other touches include complimentary decanters of port.

★ House Hotel
BOUTIQUE HOTEL €€

(☑ 091-538 900; www.thehousehotel.ie; Spanish Pde; d €205-285; 🛜) Inside a former warehouse in the liveliest part of the city, Galway's hippest hotel has a stunning setting with retro-styled furnishings and modern art, accented with bold shades like fuchsia pink. The 40 soundproofed rooms are small but plush, with vivid colour schemes and quality fabrics. Bathrooms come with toiletries by Irish designer Orla Kiely.

Adare Guesthouse
GUESTHOUSE €€

(☑ 091-582 638; www.adareguesthouse.ie; 9 Father Griffin Pl; s/d/f €75/130/150; 🅿 🛜) 🍃 Overlooking a football pitch and children's playground, this beautifully kept guesthouse has generously sized rooms and service that runs like clockwork. Sift through 16, often organic, menu choices at breakfast including French toast with caramelised plums, smoked salmon and scrambled eggs, and buttermilk pancakes with honeyed pears.

Ardawn House
B&B €€

(☑ 091-568 833; www.ardawnhouse.com; College Rd; s/d/tr/f €55/95/140/190; 🅿 🛜) Green shrubs frame the front door of this red-brick house towards the end of the B&B-lined College Rd strip. Inside, antique-style furniture sits in elegant, sparingly decorated bedrooms, while at breakfast the homemade preserves are served amid gleaming silverware and china plates.

Residence Hotel
BOUTIQUE HOTEL €€

(☑ 091-569 600; www.theresidencehotel.ie; 14 Quay St; d/tr from €139/169; 🛜) The Residence is surrounded by Quay St's music-filled pubs. Its 20 rooms are small but strikingly decorated, with street-art-style murals above the beds. Amenities include streaming TV service, pod espresso machines and luxury smellies.

Stop
B&B €€

(☑ 091-586 736; www.thestopbandb.com; 38 Father Griffin Rd; s/d/tr/f from €60/110/150/200; 🛜) Done up with contemporary artworks, stripped floorboards and bold colours, this design-conscious B&B delivers snug rooms where aesthetically pleasing space-saving tricks include hangers instead of wardrobes and streamlined work desks. Gourmet

Fresh oysters
MARIAKOVALEVA/SHUTTERSTOCK ©

breakfast includes freshly squeezed orange juice and there's a handy supermarket right across the street.

St Judes
B&B €€

(☏091-521 619; www.st-judes.com; 110 Lower Salthill Rd; s/d €98/130; P ☏) In this elegant, double-fronted 1920s stone manor house, three individually furnished rooms feature antique-style chairs, polished floorboards and gleaming bathrooms. It's set in a peaceful residential area to the west of the city centre.

St Martins
B&B €€

(☏091-568 286; 2 Nun's Island Rd; s/d €55/85; ☏) The nearest thing to staying with your own Irish relatives is checking into this welcoming B&B. Run by warm-hearted Mary, the impeccably kept older-style house has a gorgeous flower-filled garden overlooking the rushing River Corrib, and four cosy rooms complete with hot-water bottles.

Huntsman Inn
INN €€

(☏091-562 849; www.huntsmaninn.com; 164 College Rd; r €130-140; P ☏) On Lough Atalia, 1.5km northeast of central Galway, the Huntsman suits those who'd rather not stay in the city's busy heart. Its 12 rooms are streamlined and contemporary, with generous bathrooms. There's a well-regarded restaurant and bar serving craft beers; the terrific gourmet breakfasts are extra (€8 to €11).

★ Glenlo Abbey Hotel
HISTORIC HOTEL €€€

(☏091-519 600; www.glenloabbeyhotel.ie; Kentfield Bushy Park, off N59; d €357-448, ste €538-984; ☏) Set on the shores of Lough Corrib, 4km northwest of Galway, this 1740-built stone manor is the ancestral home of the Ffrench family, one of Galway's 14 tribes. Exceptionally preserved period architecture is combined with antique furnishings, sumptuous marble bathrooms, duck-down duvets and king-sized pillows. Breakfasts are lavish, while the hotel's fine-dining Pullman Restaurant (p60) occupies original *Orient Express* train carriages.

The vast grounds include a never-completed abbey with a walled garden, started by the family in 1790, as well as a nine-hole golf course (green fees €45) – the fourth hole sits on an island in the lough that's reached by a bridge. Booking a week in advance, online, brings 10% off the standard price.

G Hotel
DESIGN HOTEL €€€

(☏091-865 200; www.theghotel.ie; Wellpark, Old Dublin Rd; d €355-435, ste €515-1550; P ✳ ☏) Contrasting with its business-complex location near Lough Atalia, the stunning G Hotel has avant-garde interiors designed by Galwegian milliner-to-the-stars Philip Treacy, including a grand salon with 300 suspended silver balls, a Schiaparelli-pink cocktail lounge, and an award-winning restaurant with huge, seashell-shaped, purple banquettes. Shell-motif cushions feature in the sand-toned rooms; you can watch TV from the bathtub of most suites.

The on-site spa looks out on a bamboo-planted forest.

Kids get a personalised cookie with milk on arrival. Valet parking is free.

✖ Eating

Seafood is Galway's speciality, and Galway Bay oysters star on many menus. The smorgasbord of eating options ranges from its wonderful market (p53) to adventurous new eateries redefining Irish cuisine, and a burgeoning restaurant scene in the West End.

★ Sheridans Cheesemongers
DELI €

(☏091-564 829; www.sheridanscheesemongers. com; 14 Churchyard St; platters €9-18; ⊙shop 10am-6pm Mon-Fri, 9am-6pm Sat, wine bar 1pm-midnight Wed-Fri, noon-midnight Sat, 5pm-midnight Tue & Sun) Heavenly aromas waft from this fabulous cheesemongers filled with superb local and international cheeses. But the real secret is up a narrow flight of stairs at its wonderfully convivial wine bar. Sample from an Italian-influenced wine list while nibbling on platters of cheeses and charcuterie.

Urban Grind
CAFE €

(☑ 091-375 000; www.urbangrind.ie; 8 West William St; dishes €3.50-8.50; ⊙ 8am-6pm Mon-Fri, 9am-6pm Sat) Creative hub Urban Grind whips up fantastic breakfasts (cinnamon porridge; organic ciabatta with grilled chorizo and poached egg) and lunches (black- and white-bean tortilla with avocado and lime mayo; glazed beef brisket with horseradish relish), and brews some of Galway's best coffees and loose-leaf teas. Craft beers and boutique wines are served until 11pm Thursday to Saturday in summer.

Dough Bros
PIZZA €

(☑ 091-395 238; www.thedoughbros.ie; Middle St; pizza €9-12; ⊙ noon-9.30pm Sun-Wed, to 10pm Thu-Sat; ☎) Beginning life as a food truck, this wood-fired pizza maker has found a permanent home. The bright-green-fronted space overflows with regulars, including plenty of students, who come for its perfect crusts, fresh, flavour-loaded toppings, craft beers and casual vibe. It doesn't take bookings, but you can order pizzas to take away.

Java's
BISTRO €

(☑ 091-533 330; 17 Upper Abbeygate St; mains €7.50-8.50; ⊙ 11am-midnight Sun-Wed, to 1am Thu-Sat; ☑) We may be in western Ireland, but this is as northern France as they come. In this authentic Breton crêperie, savoury and sweet French pancakes have fillings ranging from goat's cheese with lardons, to pear with salted caramel. The cracking Irish breakfast crêpe comes with black pudding.

TGO Falafel Bar
VEGETARIAN €

(☑ 091-865 924; 11 Mary St; mains €7-9; ⊙ noon-9pm; ☑) 🌿 Galway's hipsters, vegetarians and vegans love the street-food creations rustled up by this ethics-conscious relative newcomer, thanks to fresh, flavourful vegan burgers, 'not dogs', beetroot arancini and carrot gravlax. Eat upstairs or take away.

Tuco's Taqueria
TACOS €

(☑ 091-563 925; www.tuco.ie; 6 Upper Abbeygate St; dishes €7-8; ⊙ noon-9pm; ☑) At this student favourite, you first choose from tacos, burritos or enchiladas, then select your fillings (meat, vegetarian or vegan), extras (guacamole, sour cream etc) and finally your salsa: Smokie Chipotle (hot), Roja (hotter) or Tuco's Terror (hottest; have a drink handy!).

Food 4 Thought
VEGETARIAN €

(☑ 091-565 854; 5 Lower Abbeygate St; mains €6-12; ⊙ 7.30am-5.30pm Mon-Fri, 8am-6pm Sat, 12.30-4.30pm Sun; ☎☑) Besides providing organic, vegetarian and vegan sandwiches, savoury scones and wholesome dishes such as cashew-nut roast, this place is great for finding out about energy workshops and yoga classes around town. The free filter coffee refills are plentiful.

★ Cava Bodega
TAPAS €€

(☑ 091-539 884; www.cavarestaurant.ie; 1 Middle St; tapas €7-14; ⊙ 5-10pm Mon-Thu, 4-11pm Fri, noon-11.30pm Sat, noon-9.30pm Sun; ☑) More than 50 regional Spanish tapas dishes are given a gourmet twist by star chef JP McMahon, whose other ventures include Michelin-starred Aniar (p60). Showstoppers include turf-smoked salmon, duck fritter with seaweed jam and a harissa-infused Connemara mountain lamb, along with over 100 Spanish wines.

★ John Keogh's
GASTROPUB €€

(Lock Keeper; ☑ 091-449 431; www.johnkeoghs.ie; 22 Upper Dominick St; mains €11-24; ⊙ kitchen 5-9pm Mon-Fri, 1-9pm Sat & Sun) Dark-wood panelling, snugs, stained glass, antique mirrors, book-lined shelves and blazing open fires set the scene for standout gastropub fare. John Keogh's doesn't take reservations, so arrive early to dine on mussels with home-baked soda bread and garlic aioli, or Irish oysters with a Guinness shot.

★ Oscar's
SEAFOOD €€

(☑ 091-582 180; www.oscarsseafoodbistro.com; Upper Dominick St; mains €16-30; ⊙ 5.30-9.30pm Mon-Sat) The menu changes daily at this outstanding seafood restaurant but it

---

GALWAY'S WEST END

For many Galwegians, the West End is the real Galway. Sitting just west of the River Corrib, the cluster of cafes, bistros, pubs and independent shops has an even more bohemian vibe than the rest of the city (which is saying something). Begin explorations by strolling over Wolfe Tone Bridge, cutting right up Raven Tce, into Upper Dominick St and on from there.

might include monkfish poached in saffron and white wine and served with cockles, seaweed-steamed Galway Bay lobster with garlic-lemon butter, or lemon sole with samphire. The intensely flavoured fish soup is a delight.

★ Ard Bia at Nimmo's   IRISH €€

(☑ 091-561 114; www.ardbia.com; Spanish Arch, Longwalk; cafe dishes €7-12, dinner mains €20-28; ⊙ cafe 10am-3.30pm Mon-Fri, to 3pm Sat & Sun, restaurant 6-9pm; ☑) ⬥ Casually hip Ard Bia ('High Food' in Irish) is decorated with works by local artists and upcycled vintage furniture. Organic, local, seasonal produce (some foraged) features firmly – you might sample Cork monkfish, Burren smoked haddock or Galway goat's yoghurt. Opt for the upstairs restaurant or a street-level cafe serving flavour-packed breakfasts, brunches and lunches.

Kai   MODERN IRISH €€

(☑ 091-526 003; www.kaicaferestaurant.com; 20 Sea Rd; mains lunch €12, dinner €19-28; ⊙ cafe 9.30am-3pm Mon-Fri, 10.30am-3pm Sat, restaurant 6.30-10.30pm Tue-Sat; ☎) Set in an olive-green building with exposed stone, bare timbers, fresh flowers and a glass-roofed atrium, this rustic West End spot is a fantastic place for daytime coffee, gourmet sandwiches and salads, and craft beer. Or come for adventurous evening meals such as monkfish with madras broth, perhaps followed by saffron sorbet. Reserve for dinner.

McDonagh's   FISH & CHIPS €€

(☑ 091-565 001; www.mcdonaghs.net; 22 Quay St; cafe & takeaway mains €7-16, restaurant mains €15-30; ⊙ cafe & takeaway noon-11pm Mon-Sat, 2-9pm Sun, restaurant 5-10pm Mon-Sat) A trip to Galway isn't complete without a meal here. Galway's best fish-and-chip shop fries up shoals of battered cod, plaice, haddock, whiting and salmon, accompanied by homemade tartar sauce. It's divided into two parts, with a takeaway counter and sociable cafe where diners sit elbow-to-elbow at long communal wooden tables, and a more upmarket restaurant.

Kasbah   BISTRO €€

(☑ 085 734 0164; www.kasbahwinebar.ie; 2 Quay St; mains €5-28; ⊙ food served 5-11.30pm Wed-Thu, 5pm-12.30am Fri, noon-4pm Sat) Set beside Galway's famous Tigh Neachtain pub (and also providing its bar food), the Kasbah flies the flag for fresh, locally sourced ingredients. So you might be munching on creamy Atlantic chowder at lunch, or on Roscommon Black Angus rib-eye steak for dinner. They're winners either way.

Outside food-serving hours the wine bar is open until 12.30am on Saturday, and 11.30pm on Sunday.

Quay Street Kitchen   IRISH €€

(☑ 091-865 680; The Halls, Quay St; mains €12-22; ⊙ noon-10pm; ☎☑) Vegetarian and vegan dishes such as beer-battered organic tofu are a highlight of this small, busy restaurant on bustling Quay St. It also caters well for seafood fans (cider-steamed Connemara mussels, potted crab on crusty bread) and carnivores (Irish lamb shanks, beef and Guinness stew).

★ Loam   GASTRONOMY €€€

(☑ 091-569 727; www.loamgalway.com; Fairgreen Rd; 2/3/7/9 courses €45/55/119/159; ⊙ 6-10pm Tue-Sat) ⬥ Enda McEvoy is one of the most groundbreaking chefs in Ireland today (with a Michelin star to prove it), producing inspired flavour combinations from home-grown, locally sourced or foraged ingredients: dried hay, fresh moss, edible flowers, wild oats, forest gooseberries, Salthill sea vegetables and hand-cut peat (which McEvoy uses in his extraordinary peat-smoked ice cream).

The on-site wine bar opens at 5pm and closes at 10pm Tuesday to Saturday.

★ Pullman Restaurant   FRENCH €€€

(☑ 091-519 600; www.glenloabbeyhotel.ie; Glenlo Abbey Hotel, Kentfield Bushy Park, off N59; 2/3 courses €61/69; ⊙ 6.30-10pm daily Mar-Oct, 6.30-9.30pm Fri & Sat Nov–early-Feb; ☑) One of the two original 1927 *Orient Express* train carriages at Glenlo Abbey Hotel (p58) was used in the filming of Agatha Christie's *Murder on the Orient Express* and was also part of Winston Churchill's 1965 funeral cortège. Sepia lamps, inlaid wood panelling, plush upholstery, white tablecloths and piped 1940s and 1950s music create an impossibly romantic setting for fine dining.

Expect dishes such as broth with bladderwrack, miso and mussels, and duck with fermented gooseberry and trout caviar. Vegetarians will delight in the entire menu devoted to their needs.

★ Aniar   IRISH €€€

(☑ 091-535 947; www.aniarrestaurant.ie; 53 Lower Dominick St; 6/8/10 courses €72/89/99, with wine pairings €107-169; ⊙ 6-9.30pm Tue-Thu, 5.30-9.30pm Fri & Sat) ⬥ Terroir specialist Aniar is passionate about the flavours and food producers of Galway and west Ireland. Owner and chef JP McMahon's multicourse tasting menus have earned him a Michelin star, yet the casual spring-green dining space remains refreshingly down to earth. The wine list favours small producers. Reserve at least a couple of weeks in advance.

To discover the secrets behind classic and contemporary Irish cuisine, book a course at the on-site Aniar Boutique Cookery School.

🍷 Drinking & Nightlife

Galway's pub selection is second to none. The city is awash with traditional pubs offering live music, along with stylish wine and cocktail bars. Expect throngs of revellers, especially on weekends and throughout the summer.

Look out for craft beers by local success story Galway Hooker (www.galwayhooker. ie), named for the iconic local fishing boats, on tap around town.

The city's West End (p59) has a lively bar scene, popular with locals.

★**Tigh Neachtain** PUB
(www.tighneachtain.com; 17 Upper Cross St; ⊙11.30am-midnight Mon-Thu, to 1am Fri, 10.30am-1am Sat, 12.30-11.30pm Sun) Painted a bright cornflower blue, this 19th-century corner pub – known simply as Neáchtain's (*nock*-tans) or Naughtons – has a wraparound terrace for watching Galway's passing parade, and a timber-lined interior with a roaring open fire, snugs and atmosphere to spare. Along with perfectly pulled pints of Guinness and 130-plus whiskeys, it has its own range of beers brewed by Galway Hooker.

★**Tig Cóilí** PUB
(☑091-561 294; www.tigcoiligalway.com; Mainguard St; ⊙10.30am-11.30pm Mon-Thu, to 12.30am Fri & Sat, 12.30-11pm Sun) Two live *céilidh* (traditional music and dancing session) a day (at 6pm and 9.30pm) draw the crowds to this authentic fire-engine-red pub just off High St. Decorated with photos of those who have played here, it's where musicians go to get drunk or drunks go to become musicians...or something like that. A gem.

★**Garavan's** PUB
(☑091-562 537; www.garavans.ie; 46 William St; ⊙11am-11.30pm Mon-Thu, to 12.30am Fri & Sat, 12.30-11pm Sun) Irish whiskeys are the speciality of this genteel old boozer. Incredible 'tasting platters' generally cost €11 to €14 –

LEARN TO COOK MICHELIN-STYLE

Run by JP McMahon, owner/chef of Michelin-starred Aniar restaurant, the themes of the inspiring day-long courses at **Aniar Boutique Cookery School** (☑091-535 947; www.aniar restaurant.ie; 53 Lower Dominick St; day courses €225) include tapas, dinner parties, fish, bread and wild food. Prepare to make your own butter and cheese, cure meat and fish, and pickle your own veg. Lunch and a glass of wine are included; bring a container to take your creations away.

Other options include a six-session Understanding Food course (€500), and day-long courses on contemporary Irish cooking, gastropub classics, and the perfect Christmas dinner.

choices include an Irish Writers' platter, featuring the favourite tipples of Samuel Beckett, James Joyce and WB Yeats. Or splash out on the Grand Masters' platter (€95), with an 18-year-old blended Kilbeggan, 26-year-old Teeling single malt gold reserve and 1964 Dungourney pure pot still. Look out for its whiskey-tasting events.

★**Crane Bar** PUB
See p18.

O'Connor's PUB
(☑091-523 468; www.oconnorsbar.com; Upper Salthill Rd, Salthill; ⊙7.30pm-late) Antiques fill every nook, cranny, wall and ceiling space of this 1942-established pub: clocks, crockery, farming implements, gas lights, sewing machines, fishing equipment, a stag's head and an almost life-size statue of John Wayne from *The Quiet Man*. Trad music and singalongs take place nightly.

Chalked blackboards feature quips including that the closest the pub gets to serving food is 'whiskey soup with ice croutons'.

Buddha Bar COCKTAIL BAR
(☑091-563 749; www.buddhabar.ie; 14 Mary St; ⊙5-11.30pm Mon, Wed & Thu, to 12.30am Fri & Sat, to 1am Sun) Neighbouring the **Asian Tea House** (☑091-563 749; www.asianteahouse. ie; 15 Mary St; mains €11-24; ⊙5-10.30pm; 🌶), this lantern-lit bar decorated with Buddha statues mixes inventive cocktails such as the Shanghai Kiss (passion-fruit liqueur, sake,

mango-infused vodka and orange juice) and Lotus Espresso (vanilla-infused vodka, coffee, Kahlúa and cinnamon), and serves five different Asian beers.

Nova
LGBTQI+

(☑091-725 693; www.novabargalway.com; 1 West William St; ◷4-11.30pm Mon-Thu, 3pm-2am Fri, noon-2am Sat, 12.30-11.30pm Sun; 📶) Rainbow flags and motifs adorn Galway's premier LGBTQI+ bar, where Wednesday is student night, DJs spin dance music on Friday, Saturday brings drag acts, and cocktails are suggestively named.

O'Connell's
PUB

(☑091-563 634; www.oconnellsbargalway.com; 8 Eyre Sq; ◷10.30am-11.30pm Mon-Thu, to 12.30am Fri & Sat, 12.30-11pm Sun) Right on Eyre Sq, this traditional, garrulous pub has a great, huge heated beer garden, which is home to two outdoor bars and regular music events. Original floor tiles, stained-glass windows and a pressed-tin ceiling are among its preserved features; historical photos line the walls.

From Thursday to Saturday the Dough Bros (p59) serve pizza in the garden.

King's Head
PUB

(☑091-566 630; www.thekingshead.ie; 15 High St; ◷11am-11.30pm Sun-Thu, to 2am Fri & Sat) Sprawling over three floors, this vast, ancient pub dating from the 13th century has medieval details including cut-stone windows, fireplaces and the walls of Bank's Castle. There are live events nightly.

Monroe's Tavern
PUB

(☑091-583 397; www.monroes.ie; 14 Upper Dominick St; ◷10am-11.30pm Mon-Sat, noon-11.30pm Sun) Often photographed for its classic two-storey black-and-white facade, Monroe's has been at the heart of local nightlife for more than 50 years. Expect a buzzing vibe, live music nightly and an eclectic range of gigs.

Bierhaus
BAR

(☑091-376 944; www.bierhausgalway.com; 2 Henry St; ◷4pm-midnight Sun-Thu, to 1am Fri & Sat) At any one time 20 stouts, ales, Pilsners, wheat beers and ciders from around Europe rotate on the taps of this beer specialist, in addition to over 60 bottled varieties. There are also beer-based and traditional cocktails. Soak them up with snacks such as smoked mackerel po' boys.

Róisín Dubh
PUB

See p18.

☆ Entertainment

Most pubs in Galway have live music at least a couple of nights a week, whether in an informal trad session or a headline act. Róisín Dubh is the best place for new bands; Tig Cóilí (p61) excels at trad sessions.

★ Druid Performing Arts Company
THEATRE

(☑091-568 660; www.druid.ie; Druid Lane) Internationally renowned, the Druid Performing Arts Company was established in 1975 and is famed for staging experimental works by young Irish playwrights, as well as new adaptations of classics. When it's not touring, its Galway home is the Mick Lally Theatre, situated in an old tea warehouse.

Town Hall Theatre
THEATRE

(☑091-569 777; www.tht.ie; Courthouse Sq) With a 400-seat main auditorium and 52-seat studio space, the Town Hall Theatre features Broadway and West End shows, orchestras, dance and occasional films.

🛍 Shopping

Speciality shops dot Galway's narrow streets, stocking cutting-edge fashion, Irish woollens, outdoor clothing and equipment, local jewellery, books, art and, of course, music.

★ Charlie Byrne's Bookshop
BOOKS

(☑091-561 766; www.charliebyrne.com; Cornstore, Middle St; ◷9am-6pm Mon-Wed & Sat, to 8pm Thu & Fri, noon-6pm Sun) A civic treasure, the rambling rooms at Charlie Byrne's are crammed with over 100,000 new, secondhand, thirdhand, discounted and out-of-print books,

---

CLADDAGH RINGS

The fishing village of Claddagh has long been subsumed into Galway's city centre, but its namesake rings survive as a timeless reminder.

Popular with people of Irish descent everywhere, the rings depict a heart (symbolising love) between two outstretched hands (friendship), topped by a crown (loyalty). Jewellery shops selling Claddagh rings include Ireland's oldest, **Thomas Dillon's Claddagh Gold** (☑091-566 365; www.claddaghring.ie; 1 Quay St; ◷10am-5pm Mon-Sat, noon-4pm Sun).

including a trove of Irish interest (and Irish language) fiction and nonfiction. Look out for events including book launches and storytelling sessions.

Hazel Mountain Chocolate CHOCOLATE
(www.hazelmountainchocolate.com; Middle St; ⊙11am-6.30pm) Truffles using Burren-produced Hazel Mountain chocolate (☑065-707 8847; www.hazelmountainchocolate.com; Oughtmama, off L1014; tour adult/child €15/10; ⊙shop 10am-5pm, tour days vary) are made on-site daily at this airy, contemporary shop behind a duck-egg-blue facade. It doubles as a cacao brew-bar serving its signature hot chocolate with toasted marshmallows and sweet treats such as chocolate-rhubarb brownies and chocolate-coffee cake with cardamom glaze.

Judy Greene's ARTS & CRAFTS
(☑091-561 753; www.judygreenepottery.com; Kirwan's Lane; ⊙9.30am-6pm Mon-Sat) Hand-thrown pottery by Galway artist Judy Greene incorporates designs inspired by Ireland's flora and landscapes. Also displayed in her boutique are jewellery items made from Connemara green marble, plus clothing and artworks by Irish artists and designers.

P Powell & Sons MUSICAL INSTRUMENTS
(☑091-562-295; www.powellsmusic.ie; 53 William St; ⊙9am-5.30pm Mon-Thu & Sat, to 6pm Fri, 1.30-5.30pm Sun) You can pick up everything from bodhráns (hand-held goatskin drums) and harmonicas to tin whistles and sheet music at this wonderfully traditional crimson-coloured shop, with black trim and letters picked out in gold.

Kiernan Moloney Musical Instruments MUSICAL INSTRUMENTS
(☑091-566 488; www.moloneymusic.com; 17 High St; ⊙10am-6pm Tue-Thu, to 7pm Fri, to 5.30pm Sat) Stringed instruments including fiddles and harps are the speciality of this dealer in fine instruments, which handles sales, rentals and repairs. It also stocks a small range of wind instruments. The shop sometimes opens on Sunday and Monday.

It's on the 1st floor; duck into the alley, then take the stairs immediately on the right.

ℹ️ Information

Galway's large, efficient **tourist office** (☑1850 230 330; www.discoverireland.ie; Forster St; ⊙9am-5pm Mon-Sat) can help arrange tours and has plentiful information on the city and region.

Nimmo's (p60), Spanish Arch
KIT LEONG/SHUTTERSTOCK ©

ℹ️ Getting Around

BICYCLE

Galway's Coca-Cola Zero bike-share scheme (www.bikeshare.ie/galway.html) has 22 stations around town and 195 bikes. For visitors, €3 (with €150 deposit) gets you a three-day pass. Otherwise, the first 30 minutes of each hire is free; up to two hours costs €1.50.

On Yer Bike (☑091-563 393; www.onyourbike cycles.com; 42 Prospect Hill; per day from €25; ⊙9.30am-6.30pm Mon-Fri, 11am-4pm Sat) Offers bike hire, sales and repairs.

West Ireland Cycling (☑087 205 6904; www.westirelandcycling.com; Unit 1, Bridgewater Court, Fairhill Rd; bike rental per day/week €20/125; ⊙9.30am-6pm Apr-Sep, closed Sun Oct-Mar) Rents mountain, electric, racing and touring bikes as well as accessories like child trailers, children's seats and panniers. It also organises seven-day, self-guided bike tours throughout the region (€825 including accommodation).

BUS

You can walk to almost everything in Galway, including out to Salthill, but you'll also find frequent buses departing from Eyre Sq.
For **Salthill**, take Bus Éireann bus 401 (€2, 15 minutes).

CAR & MOTORCYCLE

Parking on Galway's streets is metered. There are several multistorey and pay-and-display car parks around town – look out for 24-hour parking deals. Traffic jams can be lengthy during peak hours.

TAXI

Taxi ranks are located on **Eyre Sq**, on **Bridge St** and next to the bus and train **stations** (Station Rd). Alternatively, order one from **City Taxis** (☑ 091-525 252; www.citytaxisgalway.com; ☺ 24hr).

ARAN ISLANDS

Easily visible from the coast of Counties Galway and Clare, the rocky, wind-buffeted Aran Islands have a desolate beauty that draws countless day trippers. Visitors who stay longer experience the sensation that they're far further removed from the Irish mainland than the 40-minute ferry ride or 10-minute flight would suggest.

An extension of the limestone escarpment that forms The Burren in Clare, the islands have shallow topsoil scattered with wildflowers, grass where livestock grazes and jagged cliffs pounded by surf. Ancient forts here are some of the oldest archaeological remains in Ireland.

Inishmore (Inis Mór) is the largest island and home to the only town, Kilronan. Inishmaan (Inis Meáin) preserves its age-old traditions and evokes a sense of timelessness. Inisheer (Inis Oírr), the smallest island, has a strong trad culture.

History

Little is known about the people who built the massive Iron Age stone structures on Inishmore and Inishmaan. Commonly referred to as 'forts', they are believed to have served as pagan religious centres. Folklore holds that they were built by the Firbolgs, a people who invaded Ireland from Europe in prehistoric times.

It's thought that people came to the islands to farm, a major challenge given the rocky terrain. Early islanders augmented their soil by hauling seaweed and sand up from the shore and fished the surrounding waters on long *currachs*, which remain a symbol of the Aran Islands.

Early Christianity

Christianity reached the islands remarkably early, and some of the oldest monastic settlements were founded by St Enda (Éanna) in the 5th century. Enda appears to have been an Irish chief who converted to Christianity and spent some time studying in Rome before seeking out a suitably remote spot for his monastery.

From the 14th century, control of the islands was disputed by two Gaelic families, the O'Briens and the O'Flahertys. The English took over during the reign of Elizabeth I, and in Cromwell's times a garrison was stationed here.

Modern Isolation

In the 1600s conflicts brought destruction and disruption to Galway city. As its importance as a port waned, so did the fortunes of the Aran Islands, which relied on the city for trade. Their isolation meant that islanders maintained a traditional lifestyle well into the 20th century. Up to the 1930s, people wore traditional Aran dress: bright red skirts and black shawls for women, and baggy woollen trousers and waistcoats with *crios* (colourful belts) for men. The classic heavy cream-coloured Aran sweater, featuring complex patterns, originated here, and is still hand-knitted on the islands.

Air services began in 1970, changing island life forever, and today fast ferries make a quick (if sometimes rough) crossing.

Farming has all but died out on the islands and tourism is now the primary source of income. While Irish remains the official tongue, most locals speak English with visitors and converse with each other in Irish.

Inishmore

POP 762

Today, tourism turns the wheels of the island's economy: from May to September tour vans greet each ferry and flight, offering a ride around the sights.

◉ Sights

★ **Dun Aengus**   HISTORIC SITE
(Dún Aonghasa; ☑ 099-61008; www.heritage ireland.ie; adult/child €5/3; ☺ 9.30am-6pm Apr-Oct, to 4pm Nov-Mar) Standing guard over Inishmore, Dun Aengus, 7km west of Kilronan, has three massive drystone walls that run right up to sheer drops to the ocean below. Originally built around 1100 BC, it was refortified around 700 AD and is protected by remarkable *chevaux de frise*, fearsome and densely packed defensive limestone spikes. Displays at its small **visitor centre** provide context and a 900m walkway wanders uphill to the fort itself.

Inishmore

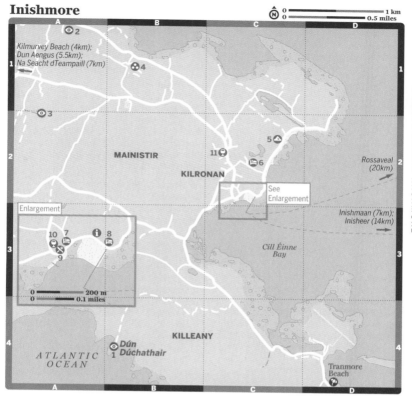

Inishmore

Powerful swells pound the 87m-high cliff face. A complete lack of railings or other modern additions that would spoil this incredible site means that you can not only go right up to the cliff's edge, but also potentially fall to your doom below – take care.

★ **Dún Dúchathair**   HISTORIC SITE
(Black Fort) **FREE** Many locals pick this ruined ancient fort, dating from the Iron Age or early medieval period, as their favourite Inishmore historic sight. It's dramatically perched on a clifftop promontory 2km southwest of Kilronan with terraced walls up to 6m high surrounding the remains of a *clochán* (early Christian beehive-shaped hut). Its name, meaning the Black Fort, comes from the dark limestone prevalent on this part of the island.

Dún Eochla
HISTORIC SITE

FREE Atop the island's highest point, at 100m, historic fort Dún Eochla has a double ring of circular walls, and is thought to date from the early medieval era. It's signposted 2.8km west of Kilronan.

Teampall Chiaráin
RUINS

(Church of St Kieran) The highlight of this small church is on the eastern side – a beautifully carved boundary cross with a circular hole at the top. It was possibly used as a sundial; drawing an item of clothing through the hole is said to bring fertility and good luck. It's thought the church was founded in the 12th century by St Kieran (aka St Ciarán), who studied under St Enda and later established his own monastery at Clonmacnoise.

Teampall Chiaráin is set 1.5km northwest of Kilronan.

Na Seacht dTeampaill
HISTORIC SITE

FREE The scattered early Christian ruins known as the Na Seacht dTeampaill (Seven Churches) actually comprise just two ruined churches. The biggest is the 13m by 5m Teampall Bhreacáin (St Brecan's Church), which dates from the 8th to 13th century. You'll also find monastic houses and fragments of several 8th-century high crosses.

⭐ Festivals & Events

Tedfest
CULTURAL

(www.tedfest.org; ☉ late Feb) Book a bed early if you're heading to this four-day carnival of nonsense celebrating the cult TV show *Father Ted* – it's a huge hit.

Pátrún
CULTURAL

(☉ Jun) On the last weekend of June a centuries-old, three-day festival celebrates St Enda, the island's patron saint. Prepare for Galway hooker and *currach* races, a triathlon, sandcastle competitions, loads of Irish music and dancing on the pier.

🛏 Sleeping

After the last day trippers have left in summer, the island assumes a wonderful serenity. Advance bookings are advised, particularly in high season. Many B&Bs and inns close during winter.

Kilronan Hostel
HOSTEL €

(☏ 099-61255; www.kilronanhostel.com; Kilronan; dm from €24; ☉ late Feb–late Oct; @ 🛜) You'll see Kilronan Hostel perched above Tí Joe Mac's pub (p24) even before your ferry docks

200m east at the pier. It's a friendly place with lots of pluses: squeaky-clean dorms, a harbour-view terrace complete with barbecue, a kitchen and free continental breakfast. Owner Dave will even lend you a double kayak for free.

Ard Mhuiris
B&B €

(☏ 099-61208; Kilronan; s/d €75/90; 🛜) Peacefully situated a five-minute stroll from the centre of town, Martin and Cait's very tidy B&B is last in a line of cottages before fields and then the sea. It has great ocean views. Martin can also take you on island tours by request. Cash only.

⭐ Aran Islands Camping & Glamping
CAMPGROUND €€

(☏ 086 189 5823; www.irelandglamping.ie; Frenchman's Beach; campsites per person €10, glamping hut €150-160) 🏄 At this smart, modern campground with direct access to a sweeping white-sand beach, you can stay in a beehive-shaped glamping hut inspired by an early Christian stone *clochán*. Sleeping up to four people, the nine timber huts have bathrooms, kitchenettes, double beds and pull-out sofas, along with sea views from the front decks. The site's green credentials include solar power.

Facilities for those pitching tents include a communal camp kitchen, showers and a common room. It's 750m north of Kilronan.

⭐ Kilmurvey House
B&B €€

(☏ 099-61218; www.aranislands.ie/kilmurvey-house; Kilmurvey; s/d from €60/95; ☉ Apr–mid-Oct; 🛜) There's a dash of grandeur about Kilmurvey House, where 12 spacious rooms sit in an imposing, 18th-century stone mansion. Breakfasts are convivial affairs, with homemade granola, porridge with whiskey and own-baked scones. It's a 500m stroll east to swim at pretty **Kilmurvey Beach**.

Pier House Guest House
INN €€

(☏ 099-61417; www.pierhousearan.com; Kilronan; d from €95; 🛜) You won't have time to lose your sea legs on the 50m walk from the ferry to this two-storey inn set on a small rise. The 12 rooms are decorated in rich shades of red, and come with tea- and coffee-making facilities. The sun terrace at the front is the perfect spot to watch harbour life go by.

🍴 Eating & Drinking

Seafood is widespread along with vegetables grown in organic garden plots. Most cafes and restaurants are in Kilronan, as are the pubs, which serve some excellent food. Self-caterers can pick up supplies at the town's small **Spar supermarket** (☑ 099-61203; www.spar.ie; Kilronan; ⊗ 9am-6pm Mon-Sat, to 5pm Sun; 🤖).

★ **Bayview Restaurant**   INTERNATIONAL €€
(☑ 086 792 9925; www.bayviewrestaurantinishmore.com; mains lunch €8-15, dinner €19-35; ⊗ noon-9pm; 🤖 🚼) At Bayview there's local art on the walls, and a deal of artistry on the plates. Beautifully presented dishes might feature Aran goat's cheese with baked mushroom tapenade, whole lobster, chargrilled steaks or the day's catch with bursts of coriander or lime.

Kids are well catered for. Winter hours can vary.

Teach Nan Phaidi   CAFE €€
(☑ 099-20975; Kilmurvey; mains €5-12; ⊗ 11am-5pm) At tiny, thatched Nan Phaidi, picnic tables sit in front of whitewashed walls, and happy diners tuck into award-winning treats. These might range from zesty, home-baked orange cake to fresh mackerel salad, or a flavourful beef and Guinness stew.

★ **Tí Joe Watty's Bar**   PUB
See p24.

The Bar   PUB
See p24.

Tí Joe Mac's   PUB
See p24.

🛍 Shopping

Kilmurvey Craft Village   ARTS & CRAFTS
(Kilmurvey; ⊗ hours vary) You'll see local knitters handcrafting traditional Aran sweaters at this charming collection of traditional thatched cottages. Woollens, Irish linen, carved stonework and jewellery incorporating Celtic designs are among the local arts and crafts for sale.

It tends to be open daily in the summer; check with the tourist office if you're making a special trip.

ℹ Information

The Spar supermarket has the Aran Islands' only ATM, but it's not unknown for it to run out of cash, especially in summer.

The welcoming **tourist office** (☑ 099-61263; www.aranislands.ie; Kilronan; ⊗ 10am-5pm, to 6pm Jul & Aug) is on the waterfront 50m north-west of the ferry pier in Kilronan.

ARAN GOAT CHEESE

You've encountered the produce on countless west Ireland menus; now meet the goats that make **Aran Goat Cheese** (☑ 087 222 6776; www.arangoatcheese.com; Oughill; tours €15-30) possible. Call ahead to join a tour of this tiny dairy where some 160 Nubian and Saanen goats produce 1000L of milk a week so you can sample delights like soft goat's cheese, a feta-like product and Gouda.

ℹ Getting Around

To see the island at a gentler pace, pony traps with a driver are available from Easter to September for trips between Kilronan and Dun Aengus; the return journey costs between €50 and €100 for up to four people.

Inishmaan

POP 183

You can easily walk to any place on the island, enjoying the stark scenery and sweeping views on the way. Inishmaan's down-to-earth islanders are largely unconcerned with the prospect of attracting the tourist dollar, so facilities are scarce.

◉ Sights

Dún Chonchúir   HISTORIC SITE
(Conor's Fort) FREE Glorious views of Inishmaan's limestone valleys and maze of stone walls extend from this ruined elliptical stone fort, which sits on the island's highest point. Built sometime between the 1st and 7th centuries AD, its walls reach over 6m in height.

Dún Fearbhaigh   HISTORIC SITE
FREE The well-preserved ruins of this stone fort are 200m west of the **Cill Cheannannach** church ruins; the fort similarly dates from around the 8th century.

Synge's Chair   VIEWPOINT
At the desolate western end of the island, Synge's Chair is a viewpoint at the edge of a sheer limestone cliff with the surf from Gregory's Sound booming below. The cliff ledge is often sheltered from the wind; do as Synge did and find a stone perch to take it all in. The formation is two minutes' walk from the end of the lane.

ARTISTIC ARAN

The Aran Islands have sustained a strong creative streak, partly as a means of entertainment during long periods of isolation. Artists and writers from the mainland have similarly long been drawn to the elemental nature of island life.

Dramatist JM Synge (1871–1909) spent a lot of time on the islands. His play *Riders to the Sea* (1905) is set on Inishmaan, while his renowned *The Playboy of the Western World* (1907) also draws upon his island experiences. Synge's highly readable book *The Aran Islands* (1907) is the classic account of life here and remains in print.

American Robert Flaherty came to the islands in the early 1930s to film *Man of Aran*, a dramatic account of daily life. He was something of a fanatic about the project and got most of the locals involved in its production. The film remains a classic that's deeply evocative of island life.

The noted 1996 play *The Cripple of Inishmaan*, by Martin McDonagh, involves tragic characters and a strong desire to leave the island in 1934.

Map-maker Tim Robinson has written a wonderful two-volume account of his explorations on Aran, called *Stones of Aran: Pilgrimage* and *Stones of Aran: Labyrinth*.

Local writer Liam O'Flaherty (1896–1984), from Inishmore, wrote several harrowing novels, including *Famine* (1937) and *Insurrection* (1950).

Teach Synge HISTORIC BUILDING
See p45.

Church of the Holy Mary of the Immaculate Conception CHURCH
(Séipéal Naomh Mhuire gan Smal; ⏲ 10am–7pm Apr–mid-Sep, to 5pm mid-Sep–Mar) Built in 1939, this small church has beautiful stained-glass windows designed by the studio of Harry Clarke and an altar by James Pearse (the father of Pádraig Pearse, aka Patrick Pearse, who led the Easter Rising in 1916).

🛏 Sleeping & Eating

Some B&Bs serve evening meals, usually using organic local produce. Food is also on offer at the acclaimed Inis Meáin inn and the pub, while the **shop** (⏲ 10am-6pm Mon-Fri, to 2pm Sat) sells grocery staples.

Cois Cuain B&B €€
(☎ 087 972 8796; www.coiscuain.com; s/d/f €40/80/90; ⏲ Apr-Sep) You'll get spotless rooms, a fine breakfast and a wealth of tips on exploring Inishmaan at this traditional, whitewashed stone Aran house. It's within easy striking distance of the beach, the pub and eateries, and they'll even run you a seaweed bath on request.

Tig Congaile B&B €€
(☎ 099-73085; www.bbinismeain.com; s/d from €50/80; 🛜) 🍴 The spacious rooms here have gleaming bathrooms and broad island views. An air of relaxation pervades, helped by the yoga classes and holistic massages

on offer. The restaurant (mains €16 to €30) delights in delivering freshly ground Guatemalan coffee and dishes packed with own-grown and foraged produce – potatoes scattered with seaweed, fresh fish on wild garlic. Dining times vary; book ahead.

Eco initiatives include solar power, and captured rainwater and seaweed fertiliser for the garden.

An Dún B&B €€
(☎ 087 680 6251; www.inismeainaccommodation. ie; d from €103; ⏲ Mar-Oct; 🛜) At modern An Dún the five comfortable cheery rooms come with wide sea views. Local cuisine such as pillowy potatoes (fertilised with seaweed), luscious smoked salmon and fresh local fish are served at its restaurant (three-course dinner menu €37); nonguests are welcome but need to book.

Kids under 12 aren't accepted. An Dún is at the foot of the Dún Chonchúir historic site.

★ Inis Meáin INN €€€
(☎ 086 826 6026; www.inismeain.com; d 2/3/5 nights from €1000/1350/2300; ⏲ Mar-Sep; 🛜) 🍴 Everything about Inis Meáin gives a boutique twist to Aran's wild heart. Five suites sit among curving, stacked stone walls, wraparound windows, crisp styling and cinematic views. The acclaimed restaurant (dinner at 8pm Wednesday, Friday and Saturday) is bold enough to deliver pared-down combinations of own-grown veg, freshly harvested shellfish and home-reared meat. Booking is required; four courses cost €75.

If you'd like a suite, book early – they sell out pretty much instantly when launched each October. Prices fall by as much as €750 per booking outside July and August.

Teach Ósta
PUB

(☎ 099-73003; ⏲ noon-late) A local linchpin, the island's only pub has outdoor tables with great views. Live music plays most nights in July and August, with spontaneous weekend sessions throughout the rest of the year. Pub food (mains €12 to €16) generally stops around 7pm and isn't always available in the winter months, though the bar often keeps going until the wee hours.

Shopping

★ Cniotáil Inis Meáin
CLOTHING

(Inis Meáin Knitting Co; ☎ 099-73009; www.inis meain.ie; ⏲ 10am-4pm Mon-Fri) One of the island's main employers was founded more than 40 years ago and today exports fine woollen garments – including iconic Aran sweaters – to some of the world's most exclusive shops. You can buy the same items at this factory shop (tax free for visitors from outside the EU). Call to confirm hours before visiting.

Inisheer
POP 281

The wheels of change turn very slowly here. Electricity wasn't fully reliable until 1997. Given that there's at best 15cm of topsoil to eke out a living farming, the slow conversion of the economy to tourism has been welcome. Day trippers from Doolin (as many as 1000 on a balmy summer weekend), 8km across the water, enliven the hiking paths all summer long. Facilities are still limited, however, so visitors need to come prepared.

◉ Sights & Activities

There are two, circular waymarked National Looped Trails, one of 8km, one of 13km.

Well of Enda
HISTORIC SITE

(Tobar Éanna) Some locals still carry out a pilgrimage known as the Turas to the Well of Enda (also known as Éinne or Endeus), a bubbling spring in a remote rocky expanse in the southwest. The ceremony involves, over the course of three consecutive Sundays, picking up seven stones from the ground nearby and walking around the small well seven times, putting one stone down each time, while saying the rosary until an elusive eel appears from the well's watery depths.

If, during this ritual, you're lucky enough to see the eel, it's said your tongue will be bestowed with healing powers, enabling you to literally lick wounds better.

O'Brien's Castle
HISTORIC BUILDING

See p46.

Plassy
SHIPWRECK

A steam trawler launched in 1940, the *Plassy* was thrown on to the rocks on 8 March 1960 and driven on to the island a couple of weeks later after another storm. Its cargo of whiskey was never recovered but miraculously, all on board were saved. The Tigh Ned (p70) pub has a collection of photographs and documents detailing the rescue. An aerial shot of the wreck was used in the opening sequence of the cult TV series *Father Ted*.

FATHER TED'S DIVINE INSPIRATION

Devotees of the late 1990s cult British TV series *Father Ted* might recognise Inisheer from the opening sequence showing the *Plassy* shipwreck on 'Craggy Island' – the show's fictional island setting off Ireland's west coast. However, apart from this single shot, the sitcom was mostly filmed in London studios, with additional location shots in Counties Clare, Wicklow and Dublin. Alas, the parochial house and Vaughan's Pub (p23) are nowhere to be found here (instead you'll find them in County Clare).

This hasn't stopped the Aran Islands from embracing the show as their own. Although there has been some grumbling from its smaller neighbours, Inishmore has seized upon *Ted*-mania for itself and each year hosts the wildly popular festival Tedfest (p66), when accommodation on the island fills up fast.

Meanwhile, County Clare now has a competing Father Ted Festival (p106) in Lisdoonvarna. As Ted might say: 'Oh feck!'

A country road in Connemara
OCSKAY BENCE/SHUTTERSTOCK ©

Áras Éanna
ARTS CENTRE

(☎ 099-75150; www.discoverinisoirr.com; ☺ hours vary, Jun-Sep) Inisheer's large community arts centre sits out on an exposed stretch of the northern side of the island and hosts visiting artist events, cultural programs and performances.

Festivals & Events

Craiceann
MUSIC
See p25.

🛏 Sleeping & Eating

Book well in advance in summer and especially during Craiceann (p25) week in June.

Seafood is the island's speciality. Pubs tend to serve food, but confirm opening hours, particularly outside the Doolin ferry season (mid-March to October). Some places only accept cash and Inisheer has no ATM, so plan ahead.

Brú Radharc Na Mara Hostel
HOSTEL €

(☎ 099-75024; www.bruhostelaran.com; dm/d €25/70; ☺ Apr-Sep; @🛜) The name translates as Seaview Hostel, and this sweet sleep spot 100m west of the pier doesn't disappoint. It offers a large kitchen, a warming fireplace, book swap, bike hire (€10 per day) and those eponymous ocean views. A continental breakfast is thrown in.

Radharc an Chaisleán
B&B €

(☎ 099-75983; Castle Village; s/d/f from €55/75/85) With views looking on to Inisheer's 14th-century O'Brien's Castle,

family-friendly Radharc an Chaisleán comes complete with an array of children's toys. It's open all year, but you'll need to book ahead in the winter.

★ South Aran House & Restaurant
B&B €€

(☎ 099-75073; www.southaran.com; s/d €65/84; ☺ Apr-Oct; 🛜) ⊘ There's an idyllic feel to this rustic B&B; lavender grows outside windows framing broad Atlantic views, and the four bedrooms have underfloor heating and wrought-iron beds. Breakfasts feature apple fritters with potato cakes and the evening restaurant (mains €17 to €25) showcases local seafood and organic produce; booking required.

Guests must be over 18. Regular events include cookery and foraging courses (from €30 per person).

Tigh Ruairí
PUB €€

(Rory's; ☎ 099-75002; d €55-94; 🛜) Rory Conneely's atmospheric digs have 20 rooms with private bathrooms and dark-wood furniture; many have views across the water. The cosy pub downstairs serves pub fare (mains €10 to €14) and hosts live music sessions in summer.

★ Teach an Tae
CAFE €

(☎ 099-75092; www.cafearan.ie; dishes €5-12; ☺ 11am-5pm May-early Nov) ⊘ Wild island raspberries and blackberries, home-grown salads, eggs from the cafe's chickens and apples from its heritage orchard are used in dishes here. Treats include net-fresh local mackerel, a herby Aran goat's cheese tart and an Irish porter cake that's laced with Guinness. Cash only.

Tigh Ned
PUB FOOD €

(☎ 099-75004; www.tighned.com; dishes €7-15; ☺ kitchen noon-4pm Apr-Oct, bar 10am-11.30pm Apr-Oct) That the daily seafood special is caught by the owner speaks volumes. Snug, welcoming Tigh Ned's has been here since 1897 dishing up inexpensive sandwiches, cottage pie and, of course, fish and chips. They're best enjoyed in Ned's harbour-view beer garden or inside listening to lively trad tunes (weekends, June to August).

🛍 Shopping

Cleas
ARTS & CRAFTS

(☎ 099-75979; www.cleas-teoranta.com; ☺ 9am-5.30pm Mon-Fri) A one-stop shop of Inisheer's traditional crafts, at Cleas you'll find willow baskets, model Aran *currachs,* brightly

WALKING INISHEER'S COAST

As well as the island's two official, circular trails, you can also circumnavigate Inisheer's 12km shoreline in about five hours, gaining a far deeper understanding of the island than from hurried visits to the main sights.

From the Inisheer ferry **pier**, walk west along the narrow road parallel to the shore and go straight on to the small fishing pier at the northwest corner of the island. Continue along the road with the shingle shore on one side and a dense patchwork of fields, enclosed by the ubiquitous stone walls, on the other. Look for tide pools and grey seals resting in the sun.

About 1km from the acute junction, turn left at the painted sign; about 100m along the paved lane is the Well of Enda (p69).

Continue southwest as the path becomes a rough track. After about 600m, head roughly south across the limestone pavement and strips of grass to the shore. Follow the gently sloping rock platform around the southwestern headland (Ceann na Faochnaí) and walk east to the **lighthouse** near Fardurris Point (two hours from the ferry pier).

Stay with the coast, turning northeast. You'll see the wreck of the *Plassy* (p69) in the distance. When necessary, use stiles to cross walls and fences around fields. Note that the grass you see grows on about 5cm of topsoil created by islanders who cleared rocks by hand and then stacked up seaweed over decades.

Head north, following the track, which then becomes a sealed road at the northern end of Lough More. Continue following the road along the northern shore of the island, past the **airstrip** (INQ).

At the airstrip you can diverge for Teampall Chaoimháin and O'Brien's Castle (p46). Otherwise rest on the lovely sands of the curving **beach** and check out the nearby **Cnoc Rathnaí**, a Bronze Age burial mound (1500 BC) that is remarkably intact considering it was submerged by sand until the 19th century, when it was rediscovered.

coloured belts and hand-harvested seaweed products.

Cleas also offers occasional basket-weaving workshops (call for details) and weekly, 1½-hour guided walks (€5), which set off from the shop at noon on Tuesdays, March to September.

❶ Information

In July and August a small **kiosk** (www.discover inisoirr.com; ◷10am-6pm Jul & Aug) at the ferry pier provides tourist information.

CONNEMARA

The name Connemara (Conamara) translates as 'Inlets of the Sea' and the roads along the peninsula's filigreed shoreline bear this out as they wind around the coves of this breathtaking stretch of Ireland's jagged west coast.

From Galway city, a slow, shore-side route passes hidden beaches and seaside hamlets. At the start of the Gaeltacht region, west of Spiddal, the scenery becomes increasingly dramatic, with parched fields rolling to fissured bays.

Connemara's starkly beautiful interior, traversed by the N59, is a kaleidoscope of rusty bogs, lonely valleys and shimmering black lakes. At its heart are the Maumturk Mountains and the pewter-tinged quartzite peaks of the Twelve Bens mountain range, with a network of scenic hiking and biking trails. Everywhere the land is laced by stone walls.

❶ Information

➡ Galway city's tourist office (p63) has lots of information on the area.

➡ Online, **Connemara Tourism** (www.connemara. ie) and **Go Connemara** (www.goconnemara.com) have region-wide info and links.

❶ Getting There & Around

Your own wheels are the best way to get off this scenic region's beaten track. Watch out for the narrow roads' stone walls and meandering Connemara sheep – characterised by their thick creamy fleece and coal-black face and legs.

The main road from Galway is the N59, which heads northwest via Oughterard to Clifden then swings northeast up to Letterfrack and Connemara National Park and on to Killary Harbour before crossing into County Mayo.

An alternative route between Galway and Clifden is via the R336 and R340; you can either join the N59 near Recess, or continue along the coast via the R342 then R341 to Roundstone, Ballyconneely and Derrygimla and on to Clifden. Side roads lead to tiny inlets, little coves and remote beaches. In the south, the low, bleak islands of Lettermore, Gorumna and Lettermullen are linked by bridges.

Inishbofin

POP 170

Situated 9km from the mainland, the tranquil island of Inishbofin measures just under 6km long by 4km wide, and its highest point is a mere 86m above sea level.

Its history is more tumultuous: St Colman exiled himself to Inishbofin in AD 665, after he fell out with the Church over its adoption of a new calendar. He set up a monastery northeast of the harbour, where the more recent ruins of a small 14th-century church still stand. Grace O'Malley, the famous pirate queen, used Inishbofin as a base in the 16th century, and Cromwell's forces captured the island in 1652, using it to jail priests and clerics.

Sights & Activities

Inishbofin offers excellent walking, cycling and horse riding.

The island has three looped routes; you can download maps for the routes from the island's Community Centre website.

The ruined 14th-century chapel on the site of St Colman's monastery is a highlight of the 8km **Cloonamore Loop**. Spectacular views over Counties Galway, Mayo and Clare feature on the 5km **Middlequarter Loop**. The 8km **Westquarter Loop** takes in the Atlantic coast, with views of the island's blowholes, sea arch and seal colony.

All three loops start and finish at the pier.

Inishbofin Heritage Museum   MUSEUM
(⊙noon-1.30pm & 2.30-5pm Easter-Sep) FREE
Inishbofin's small but evocative museum gives a comprehensive overview of the island's history. Displays include fishing, farming and tradespeople's tools as well as items from traditional Irish homes (crockery, clothing, furniture and more) and more than 200 photos of islanders over the years. Hours can vary.

Inishbofin Equestrian Centre   HORSE RIDING
(☑087 950 1545; www.inishbofinequestriancentre. com; ⊙9am-6pm) Offers horse-riding lessons (from €35 per hour) catering for all ages and abilities and treks (€30 per hour) around the island. Evening rides are possible by request.

Festivals & Events

Inishbofin Arts Festival   CULTURAL
See p40.

Sleeping & Eating

Self-caterers should stock up on the mainland, although Inishbofin's post office has a small grocery shop. There are around nine restaurants and bars, most located at the island's hotels. Many places only accept cash and the island has no ATM – come prepared.

Inishbofin Island Hostel   HOSTEL €
(☑095-45855; www.inishbofin-hostel.ie; campsites per person €12, dm/d €18/50, f €50-100; ⊙Easter-Sep) A clutch of new glamping pods (per night €50) add a bit of pizzazz at this snug 38-bed hostel, with its six-bed dorms and private rooms with shared bathroom facilities. Good amenities include a conservatory with panoramic views, self-catering kitchen, barbecue, laundry and lounge with solid-fuel stove. It's 1km east of the pier.

Inishbofin House Hotel   HOTEL €€
(☑095-45888; www.inishbofinhouse.com; d €110-140, f from €180; ⊙Apr-Sep; ☏) The emphasis in this swish modern hotel is on relaxation: a comfy bed in a serene guest room, in the library, in the large lounge overlooking a cove. Standard rooms look out on to farmland; sea-view rooms (some with balconies) cost more. Seafood is the mainstay of the hotel's restaurant (mains €18 to €30).

Inishbofin House Hotel is 400m east of the pier.

Lapwing House   B&B €€
(☑095-45996; www.inishbofin.com/bandb/lapwing. html; d from €80; ☏) Named after the local bird species that breeds on the island, this lovely family-run B&B in a whitewashed building 500m north from the pier has just two rooms (one double and one twin), each with a private bathroom. Views extend over the sheep-flecked hillside to the harbour.

Homemade breakfast pancakes come with maple syrup.

Information

The island's website (www.inishbofin.com) and **Community Centre** (☑095-45895; www.

inishbofin.com; ⊙ 9am-11pm Mon-Thu, to 5pm Fri, noon-4pm Sat & Sun; 🛜) are good resources for local information.

ℹ Getting There & Away

Ferries from Cleggan to Inishbofin take 30 to 45 minutes and are run by **Island Discovery** (☑ 095-45819; www.inishbofinislanddiscovery. com; adult/child return €20/10). In low season there are two ferries a day, increasing to three from June to August. Dolphins often swim along-side the boats, and basking sharks can often be spotted in April. Confirm ahead, as ferries may be cancelled when seas are rough.

Letterfrack & Around

POP 192

Founded by Quakers in the mid-19th century, Letterfrack (Leitir Fraic) is a crossroads with a few pubs and B&Bs. But the forested setting and nearby coast are a magnet for outdoors adventure seekers. A 4km walk to the peak of **Tully Mountain** (356m) takes 40 minutes and offers uplifting ocean views.

⊙ Sights & Activities

★**Kylemore Abbey**   HISTORIC BUILDING
(☑ 095-52001; www.kylemoreabbey.com; off N59; adult/child €13/free; ⊙ 9am-7pm Jul & Aug, 9.30am-5.30pm Sep & Oct, 9am-6pm Apr-Jun, 10am-4.30pm Nov-Mar) Photogenically perched on the shores of Pollacapall Lough, 4km east of Letterfrack, Kylemore is a crenellated 19th-century neo-Gothic fantasy. It was built for a wealthy English businessman, Mitchell Henry, who spent his honeymoon in Conne-mara. Ground-floor rooms are open to visi-tors, and you can wander down to the lake and the **Gothic church**. Admission includes entry to the extravagant **Victorian walled gardens**, around a 20-minute walk away (linked by a free shuttle bus from April to October).

★**Connemara National Park**   NATIONAL PARK
See p40.

DK Connemara Oysters   FACTORY
(☑ 087 918 6997; www.dkconnemaraoysters.com; Ballinakill Bay; adult/child €15/5; ⊙ 11am & 4pm Fri-Sun Easter-Sep) On these hour-long tours you'll get a real sense of the skill and sheer hard work that goes into producing Conne-mara's famous oysters. Then try your hand at shucking, grading and, of course, tasting them, fresh from the sea. Book ahead.

Connemara Guided Walks   WALKING
(☑ 076-100 2528; www.connemaranationalpark.ie) **FREE** National park rangers lead free guided walks from the Connemara National Park visitor centre. Themes vary and include flora, fauna, history, geology and children's activities. Check the park's online events pages for details.

🛏 Sleeping & Eating

Letterfrack has pubs and a small super-market, but there are many more dining options in Clifden.

Letterfrack Lodge   HOSTEL €
(Connemara National Park Hostel; ☑ 095-41222; off N59; dm/d/tr/q €25/90/110/160; 🅿🛜) Close to the Letterfrack crossroads, this stone-fronted hostel has spacious dorms as well as private rooms with their own bathrooms. There's a big self-catering kitchen-dining room, and friendly staff are a great source of info on walks throughout the region.

Rosleague Manor   HOTEL €€€
(☑ 095-41101; www.rosleague.com; N59; s/d €145/210, f & ste €249; ⊙ Easter–mid-Nov; 🅿🛜) Rose-pink Rosleague Manor is gloriously sited – overlooking Ballynakill Harbour and the Twelve Bens mountain range. Richly coloured rooms, furnished with antiques and original artworks, make it feel like a romantic hideaway, as do walking trails through private woods, a Victorian con-servatory and an excellent restaurant (two/ three courses €35/49). It's 2km west of Letterfrack.

Fruit, vegetables and herbs come from its own kitchen gardens.

ℹ Information

The **Connemara National Park Visitor Centre** (☑ 076-100 2528; www.connemaranationalpark. ie; off N59, Letterfrack; ⊙ 9am-5.30pm Mar-Oct) is in a beautiful setting 300m south of the Letter-frack crossroads, and offers an introduction to the park's flora, fauna and geology.

STRETCH YOUR LEGS
GALWAY

Start/Finish Spanish Arch

Distance 1.8km

Duration 2 hours

The best way to soak up Galway's convivial atmosphere is to wander its cobblestoned streets. This walk takes you from the city's medieval roots, through its cafe- and bar-lined heart to some of its finest historic buildings.

Take this walk on Trips

Spanish Arch & Medieval Walls

Framing the river east of Wolfe Tone Bridge, the Spanish Arch (1584) is thought to be an extension of Galway's medieval walls. The arch appears to have been designed as a passageway through which ships entered the city to unload goods, such as wine and brandy from Spain. Today, the lawns and riverside form a gathering place for locals and visitors on any sunny day.

The Walk ≫ A mere step from the Spanish Arch, you can't miss the modernist Galway City Museum. For cake and coffee before you go, Ard Bia, right opposite, will hit the spot beautifully.

Galway City Museum

The **Galway City Museum** (☎091-532 460; www.galwaycitymuseum.ie; Spanish Pde; ⊙10am-5pm Tue-Sat, plus noon-5pm Sun Easter-Sep) is in a glossy, glassy building that reflects the old walls. Exhibits trace aspects of daily life through Galway's history; especially good are the areas dealing with life – smelly and otherwise – during medieval times. Look for the photos of President John F Kennedy's 1963 visit to Galway, including one with dewy-eyed nuns looking on adoringly.

The Walk ≫ A few minutes' walk from here, crossing the plaza and heading up bustling Quay St, take the first right at the Quays Pub onto Druid Lane, also home to the acclaimed Druid Theatre.

Hall of the Red Earl

Back in the 13th century when the de Burgo family ran the show in Galway, Richard – the Red Earl – had a large **hall** (www.galwaycivictrust.ie; Druid Lane; ⊙9am-4.45pm Mon-Fri, 11am-3pm Sat) built as a seat of power. The hall fell into ruin and was lost until 1997 when expansion of the city's Custom House uncovered its foundations. It now gives a fascinating sense of Galway life some 900 years ago.

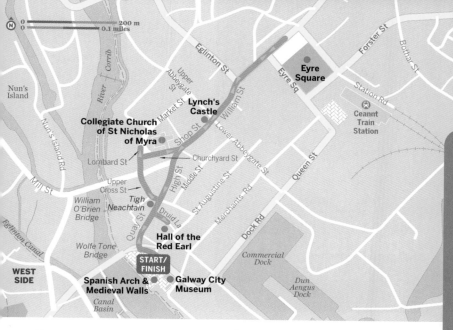

The Walk ›› Back on Quay St walk up as far as Tigh Neachtain's, and left onto Cross St where you continue for 50m. You'll spot the Church of St Nicholas on your right.

Collegiate Church of St Nicholas of Myra

Crowned by a pyramidal spire, the **Collegiate Church of St Nicholas of Myra** (☎086-389 8777; www.stnicholas.ie; Lombard St; by donation; ⏰9am-7pm Mar-Dec, to 5pm Jan & Feb) is Ireland's largest medieval parish church still in use. Dating from 1320, the church has been rebuilt and enlarged over the centuries. St Nicholas is the patron saint of sailors – Christopher Columbus reputedly worshipped here in 1477.

The Walk ›› Outside on Lombard St, head east along Churchyard St to Shop St and straight up to Eyre Sq, 600m from the church.

Eyre Square

Galway's central public square is an open space with sculptures and pathways. The eastern side is taken up almost entirely by the Hotel Meyrick, an elegant grey limestone pile. Guarding the upper side of the square, **Browne's Doorway** (1627), a classy, if forlorn, fragment is from the home of one of the city's merchant rulers.

The Walk ›› From north of the square, make your way back down Shop St. Not far down on the right-hand side you'll spot the stone facade of Lynch's Castle, now a bank.

Lynch's Castle

Considered the finest town castle in Ireland, the old stone **Lynch's Castle** (Shop St; ⏰10am-4pm Mon-Wed & Fri, to 5pm Thu) was built in the 14th century. The Lynch family was the most powerful of the 14 ruling Galway 'tribes'. Stonework on the castle's facade includes ghoulish gargoyles and many coats of arms.

The Walk ›› It may take you a while to navigate the pleasant bustle of Shop St, with its many buskers and shoppers. Return to the Spanish Arch via High St, stopping at Tigh Neachtain for a sup en route.

Counties Mayo & Sligo

Despite their natural wonders and languid charm, Counties Mayo and Sligo remain a well-kept secret, offering all of Ireland's wild, romantic beauty but without the crowds. Mayo is the more rugged of the two, whereas Sligo is more pastoral.

COUNTY MAYO

Mayo has wild beauty and haunting landscapes, but you'll find few tourists here, which means there are plenty of untapped opportunities for exploration by car, foot, bicycle or horseback. Life here has never been easy and the Potato Famine (1845–51) ravaged the county and prompted mass emigration. Consequently many people with Irish ancestry around the world can trace their roots to this once-blighted land.

Cong

POP 145

The wooded trails between the lovely old abbey and stately Ashford Castle offer a respite from crowds; continue further and you find the area is honeycombed with limestone caves, each associated with a colourful legend.

Look out for the gaunt roofless church with tower as you travel down through Ballinrobe on the way to Cong. From Cong, a gorgeous and straightforward car journey travels in a scenic loop around Lough Mask.

Sights

Ashford Castle Estate HISTORIC SITE
See p38.

Cong Abbey HISTORIC SITE
(Mainistir Chonga; ☑094-954 6542; Abbey St; ⊙dawn-dusk) FREE The evocatively weathered shell of Cong's 12th-century Augustinian abbey is scored by a cross-hatch of lines from centuries of exposure to the elements. Nevertheless, several finely sculpted features have survived, including a carved doorway, windows, lovely medieval arches and the ruined cloisters.

Pigeonhole Cave CAVE
See p38.

⚡ Activities

Corrib Cruises CRUISE
(☑087 283 0799; www.corribcruises.com; Lisloughery Pier; adult/child from €20/10) Cruises on Lough Corrib run from both Lisloughery Pier and Ashford Castle Pier, 15 minutes away by boat. A 75-minute history cruise departs each morning year-round; there are two-hour island cruises in the afternoons between June and September. They visit Inchagoill, the island at the centre of Lough Corrib with 5th-century monastic ruins.

Ashford Outdoors KAYAKING
(☑094-954 6507; www.ashfordoutdoors.com; Ashford Equestrian Centre, Ashford Castle Estate; tours from adult/child €75/55, bike rental per day from

adult/child €40/30) Pedal the shores and then paddle the waters of Ashford Castle Estate and Lough Corrib on these tours by bike, kayak, SUP, horse and pony.

🛏 Sleeping

Lakeland House
HOSTEL €

(Cong Hostel; 📞 094-954 6089; www.quietman-cong.com; Quay Rd, Lisloughrey; campsites per 2 adults €25, dm/d/f €20/55/75; 🅿 🛜) In this well-run hostel a mini-cinema screens Cong's iconic *The Quiet Man* film *every* night. The four-bed dorms and doubles are simple but bright and comfortable. You can borrow fishing rods, and there's even a freezer for your catch. Breakfast is included, except for campers.

Nymphsfield House
B&B €

(📞 094-954 6320; www.nymphsfieldhouse.com; R345, Gortaroe; s €50, d €70-80; 🛜) Just north-east of Cong (a pretty 10-minute or 1km walk), in the vicinity of several good B&Bs, this family-run B&B offers a warm welcome and a breakfast menu featuring cooked-to-order omelettes, smoked salmon and waffles. You'll also find a place to store your fishing gear.

Michaeleen's Manor
B&B €

(📞 094-954 6089; www.michaeleensmanor.com; Quay Rd, Lisloughrey; s/d/f €55/75/115; 🅿 🛜) One for fans of *The Quiet Man* film: each of 12 comfy rooms here is named after a character in the movie and is decorated with memorabilia and quotations. The lush garden even has a large fountain replica of Galway's Quiet Man Bridge. It's about 2km east of Cong.

Ryan's Hotel
HOTEL €€

(📞 094-954 6243; www.ryanshotelcong.ie; Main St; s from €85, d €110-120; 🛜) From the earth-tone checked carpets to the sketches of fishing flies on the walls, Ryan's is every inch a Lough Corrib hotel. Add a genuinely warm welcome, cosy bars, a village-centre location and a quality breakfast menu and you have a winner.

★ Lodge at Ashford Castle
HOTEL €€€

(📞 094-954 5400; www.thelodgeac.com; Quay Rd; d €289-323, ste €395-540; 🛜) Built in the 1820s by the owners of nearby, prestigious Ashford Castle, the lodge has rich, contemporary colours, plush furnishings, handmade toiletries and dreamy lake views. The suites are magnificent: some boast private terraces and mini-balconies, while others have rain showers and range over two floors.

The lodge's renowned eatery, Wilde's at the Lodge, delivers fine dining at its best.

Ashford Castle
HOTEL €€€

(📞 094-954 6003; www.ashfordcastle.com; d €675-950, ste €1725-5000; 🛜) High-end luxury, exquisite interiors and superb personalised service define Ashford Castle, once home to the Guinness family. Old-world elegance is everywhere, from the vaulted wine cellars and refined billiard room to the state-of-the-art spa. The 140-hectare estate is home to horse riding, fishing, falconry and golf, and eating options range from fine dining to afternoon tea.

🍴 Eating & Drinking

★ Hungry Monk
CAFE €

(📞 094-954 5842; Abbey St; mains €6-14; ⏰ 10am-5pm Mon-Sat Mar-Nov; 🛜) With the warmest of welcomes, this simple cafe with bright colours and artfully mismatched, distressed furniture is a perfect refuge on a misty day. Locally sourced ingredients make up the excellent sandwiches, soups and salads, the luscious cakes are homemade and the coffee is excellent.

Fennel Seed Restaurant
IRISH €€

(📞 094-954 6004; www.ryanshotelcong.ie; Main St, Ryan's Hotel; bar food €13-22, mains €16-29; ⏰ 6-9pm Mon-Sat, 1-7pm Sun) Denis Lenihan's culinary skills enjoy widespread acclaim, so make sure you don't miss the signature 'smoky bake' pie, stuffed with trout, salmon, mackerel, haddock and knockout flavour. Bar food is served in the adjoining Crowe's Nest Pub until 7pm.

★ Wilde's at the Lodge
IRISH €€€

(📞 094-954 5400; www.thelodgeac.com; Quay Rd, Lisloughrey Lodge; 5 courses €65; ⏰ 6.30-9pm Thu-Sun plus 1-3.30pm Sun; 🛜) Chef Jonathan Keane and his team forage the mussels, wild herbs and flowers that adorn the dishes at this exquisite restaurant within the vast grounds of Ashford Castle. Produce and meat come from organic local suppliers for a much-lauded, seasonally changing menu, bringing the chance to sample many dishes served on small plates.

Pat Cohan's
PUB

(📞 094-954 5620; www.patcohanbar.ie; Abbey St; ⏰ 10am-11pm) In a case of life imitating art, this one-time grocery store was disguised in the film *The Quiet Man* as the fictional Pat Cohan's. But as *The Quiet Man* craziness only grows, it has now become that pub.

ℹ Information

The **tourist office** (☑ 016-057 700; www.discover ireland.ie; Abbey St; ⊙ 9am-5pm Tue-Sat Mar-Sep, winter hours vary) is in the old courthouse building opposite Cong Abbey.

Delphi

There's a bed for most budgets at the modern, multipurpose **Delphi Resort** (☑ 095-42208; www.delphiadventureresort.com; off R335; dm €15-17, d €129, ste €199-229; ℗ @ 🛜), from standard guest rooms, loft rooms and larger suites (some with enormous timber decks) to luxury six-bed dorms with bathrooms where each bunk has its own USB charger and reading light. A cavernous pub-restaurant serves great bar food (mains €12 to €29). Spa treatments use hand-harvested seaweed and the property's own mountain spring water. There's a good **cafe** (☑ 095-42208; www.delphiadventureresort.com; Delphi Resort, off the R335; mains from €7; ⊙ 9.30am-5.30pm; 🛜) here as well.

Dwarfed by the mountainous backdrop, **Delphi Lodge** (☑ 095-42222; www.delphilodge.ie; off R335; s from €150, d €265-295, f €295, ste €295; ℗ @), a wonderful 1830s Georgian mansion beside Fin Lough, was built by the Marquis of Sligo. The 13-room country hotel features beautiful interiors, colossal 405-hectare grounds, delicious food (six-course dinner €65) and a serious lack of pretension. It's popular with fishers (half-day with fishing tutor €180) and those seeking relaxation and escape.

Westport

POP 6198

Westport is Mayo's nightlife hub, and its central location makes it a convenient and enjoyable base for exploring the county.

◉ Sights

Westport Quay, the town's harbour, is on Clew Bay, 2km west of the centre. It's a picturesque spot with shops and cafes. In town, the **Octagon** is a major landmark, punctuated by a Doric column.

Westport House   HISTORIC BUILDING
See p29.

Clew Bay Heritage Centre   MUSEUM
(☑ 098-26852; www.westportheritage.com; Westport Quay; adult/child €3/free; ⊙ 10am-5pm

Mon-Fri Jun & Sep, 10am-5pm Mon-Fri, 3-5pm Sun Jul & Aug, 10.30am-2pm Mon-Fri Oct-May) Set in a 19th-century stone building 2km west of town, this museum traces the history, customs and traditions of Westport and Clew Bay.

🏃 Activities & Tours

The area around Westport is superb for cycling, with gentle coastal routes or more challenging mountain trails to test your legs, all within a short distance of town. The Great Western Greenway, a 42km cycling route between Westport and Achill, begins 500m from the centre of town off the N59.

The tourist office (p81) has an excellent brochure detailing local walks for all skill levels.

★ Clew Bay Bike Hire   CYCLING
(☑ 098-37675; www.clewbaybikehire.ie; Distillery Rd; adult/child per day €20/15; ⊙ 9am-6pm) Offers advice on routes and trails in the area and has shops in Westport and along the Great Western Greenway in Newport, Mulranny and Achill. Its shuttle service means you can start the trail at any point and be picked up on completion (per adult/child €15/free).

During summer, it also offers half-day sea-kayaking tours (per person €60, minimum four people, private tour €130 per person).

**★ Guided Walks of
Historic Westport**   WALKING
(☑ 098-26852; www.westportheritage.com; Bridge St; per person €5; ⊙ 11am Wed Jul-Sep) Local historians lead 90-minute walks around Westport. They start at Westport's historic clock tower in the centre of town.

Westport Walking Tours   WALKING
(☑ 087 410 1363; www.westportwalkingtours.ie; from €5; ⊙ times vary) Tours of the town include two-hour walking tours, and a meander around the pick of the local pubs, sampling craft beers. Check times and departure points online.

Croagh Patrick Walking Holidays   WALKING
(☑ 098-26090; www.walkingguideireland.com; 7-day walks from €800; ⊙ Apr-Aug) Highly customisable walks in the countryside surrounding Westport that usually last seven days. You can include St Patrick's holy site and/or a beach. Fees include accommodation, breakfast and lunch.

Westport

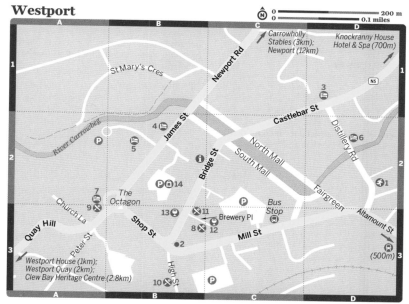

Westport

Activities, Courses & Tours

Sleeping

Eating

Drinking & Nightlife

Shopping

Clewbay Cruises   BOATING
(☑098-39192; www.clewbaycruises.com; Westport Quay; adult/child €20/10; ⊙May-Oct) Enjoy views of Clew Bay on 90-minute cruises.

Carrowholly Stables   HORSE RIDING
(☑098-27057; www.carrowholly-stables.com; near Carrowholly; per hr adult/child €30/25) All skill levels are catered for at this recommended outfit, which offers horse and pony treks on the beach and beside Clew Bay. The stables are 3km northwest of the town centre, near the village of Carrowholly.

🛏 Sleeping

Westport is Mayo's main city, and while there's an abundance of B&Bs and hotels, rooms are in short supply during summer and special events.

Old Mill Holiday Hostel   HOSTEL €
(☑098-27045; www.oldmillhostel.com; off James St; dm/d/f from €18/50/75; ☎) There's an appealing feel to the rooms in this converted stone mill. Dorms range from four to 12 bed, while the family rooms sleep up to four. The communal areas are inviting and there's a handy kitchen and laundry.

★ **St Anthony's Riverside B&B**   B&B €€
(☑098-28887; www.st-anthonys.com; Distillery Rd; s from €90, d €100-115; ℗☎) It may be in the middle of Westport, but a tall hedge and thick, twisted vines give this genteel,

19th-century B&B a tucked-away feel. Rooms have clean lines and restful, light colours, some also have Jacuzzis. There's a large garden to relax in and breakfast is excellent.

Clew Bay Hotel
HOTEL €€

(098-28088; www.clewbayhotel.com; James St; s/d from €85/130;) Some of the small but stylish rooms at this central, family-run, three-star hotel come with river views. Bathrooms and furnishings are first-rate, while the modern pub is popular for contemporary takes on classic fare. Parking costs €3 a day.

Wyatt Hotel
HOTEL €€

(098-25027; www.wyatthotel.com; The Octagon; s from €69, d €110-218; P) The Wyatt is a local landmark. Plumb in the centre of Westport, painted a sunflower yellow and stretching around one side of the central Octagon, it has been accommodating travellers in style for centuries. Standard rooms are comfortable; restyled and fresh superior rooms have large beds, walk-in showers and lavish amenities.

Prices can fall by as much as €40 per double on weekdays in low season.

Castlecourt Hotel
HOTEL €€

(098-55088; www.castlecourthotel.ie; Castlebar St; s €128, d €128-163, ste/f €180/150; @) The spacious but still cosy rooms at this grand hotel in the town centre blend contemporary style with classic elegance. It has a gym, a 20m indoor pool and a very snazzy spa.

Knockranny House Hotel & Spa
BOUTIQUE HOTEL €€€

(098-28600; www.knockrannyhousehotel.ie; off N5; r €100-160, ste €170-300; @) Open fires take the chill out of the air at this modern hotel, where more than 100 rooms and suites each feature plush classic furnishings and styles. Amenities include an indoor pool and spa facilities. Westport's centre is 1.5km west, a 15-minute walk.

✖ Eating

Westport is packed with superb restaurants and cafes: just wander along Bridge St and the little laneways off it to make some tasty discoveries. Book for dinner in summer and on weekends.

Creel
CAFE €

(098-26174; The Quay; mains €5-12; 10am-4pm Wed-Thu, 9.30am-5pm Fri-Sun) With its lively chatter, superb cakes and all-day

brunches, Creel conjures up inventive treatments with traditional Mayo ingredients. Lunch might be a warming chicken noodle soup or a vivid, seed-scattered salad; puddings span rhubarb crumble to lemon meringue pie.

★ Pantry & Corkscrew
IRISH €€

(098-26977; www.thepantryandcorkscrew.com; The Octagon; mains €17-24; 5-10pm daily May-Sep, Wed-Sun Oct-Apr;) The heart of Mayo's slow-food movement is found at this narrow storefront with a turquoise exterior and interior walls crammed with pictures. The kitchen works culinary magic with seasonal, local and organic produce to rustle up stout-braised beef, maple-glazed pork and arancini with jalapeño and Aran Islands feta. Book ahead.

The early-evening menu (5pm to 6.30pm; two/three courses €22/25) is superb value.

★ An Port Mór
IRISH €€

(098-26730; www.anportmor.com; 1 Brewery Pl; mains €14-22, 5 courses €39; 5-9pm Sun-Thu, to 9.30pm Fri & Sat;) Proprietor-chef Frankie Mallon's little restaurant packs a big punch. It's an intimate place with a series of long narrow rooms and a menu featuring gutsy flavours, excellent meats and much-lauded seafood (try the excellent Clew Bay scallops). Just about everything is procured from the region.

The two-course early-bird menu (€24), served nightly between 5pm and 6pm, is superb value.

Helm
SEAFOOD €€

(098-26398; www.thehelm.ie; The Quay; mains €12-22; 8am-9.30pm) Fittingly for a pub beside a boat-backed quay, Helm showcases the freshest Irish seafood, with chefs working with fish caught between Rossaveal in County Galway and Ballina in County Mayo. Regulars on the menu include salmon stuffed with spinach and prawns, and perfectly cooked black sole on the bone.

Sage
EUROPEAN €€

(098-56700; www.sagewestport.ie; 10 High St; mains €18-26; 5.30-9.30pm Thu-Tue;) A wave of aromas hits as you walk through the door of this stylish restaurant, artfully run by Shteryo Yurukov and Eva Ivanova. Foraged, wild and local ingredients are the mainstays, as are innovative flavour combinations – crab claws with wild garlic, a bitter coastline salad and free-range chicken with wild mushroom sauce.

There's an early-evening menu (two/three courses €22/26) and the vast majority of dishes are coeliac friendly.

Sol Rio MEDITERRANEAN €€
(📞 098-28944; www.solrio.ie; Bridge St; mains lunch €10, dinner €14-22; ⏰ cafe 9am-6pm, restaurant noon-3pm & 6-10pm; 🚲) The extensive menu here ranges from pizza and pasta to organic meat and fish. Carefully chosen ingredients are combined cleverly, whether you pause at the simple cafe downstairs or the more stylish restaurant upstairs. The deli is famous for its egg-custard pastries.

🍷 Drinking & Nightlife

Westport is thronged with pubs, many of them with regular live music.

★ Matt Molloy's PUB
(📞 098-27663; www.mattmolloy.com; Bridge St; ⏰ 12.30-11.30pm Mon-Thu, to 12.30am Fri & Sat, to 11pm Sun; 🛜) Matt Malloy, the fife player from the Chieftains, runs this old-school pub where Mayo's musical heritage comes vividly to life. Head to the back room most nights and you'll probably catch live *céilidh* (traditional music and dancing). Or perhaps a veteran musician will simply slide into a chair and croon a few classics. Great microbrews on tap add to the allure.

Gallery WINE BAR
(📞 083 109 1138; www.thegallerywestport.com; 9 Brewery Pl; ⏰ 4-11.30pm Tue-Thu, 4pm-midnight Fri, 2pm-midnight Sat) With its ranks of vinyl, twin turntables, shelves stacked with books and comfy chairs, the Gallery is the hang-out of choice for Westport's cool crowd. Add live music, board games, tapas and an array of biodynamic wines and you may stay longer than planned.

🛍 Shopping

Wandering Westport's centre, you'll discover little boutiques and a surprising number of bookshops.

Market MARKET
(James St car park; ⏰ 8.30am-1pm Thu) Fresh produce from the region.

Custom House Studios ART
(📞 098-28735; www.customhousestudios.ie; Westport Quay; ⏰ 10am-5pm Mon-Fri, 1-4.30pm Sat & Sun) Local artists display their creations at this inviting gallery, which also has special exhibitions.

ℹ Information

Mayo's main **tourist office** (📞 098-25711; www.westporttourism.com; Bridge St; ⏰ 9am-5.45pm Mon-Fri year-round, plus 10am-4pm Sat Easter-Oct) has a lot of walking and cycling info.

Achill Island

POP 2440

Achill (An Caol) has its share of history, having been a frequent refuge during Ireland's various rebellions. It's at its most dramatic during winter, when high winds and lashing seas make the island seem downright inhospitable. The year-round population, though, remains as welcoming as ever. In summer, heather, rhododendrons and wildflowers bloom, splashing the island with colour.

The village of Keel is the island's main centre of activity – which is a relative term; shops and services also cluster at the end of the bridge onto the island, at Achill Sound.

👁 Sights

Instead of following the main road (R319) from Mulranny to Achill Island, take the signposted Ocean Rd, which curves clockwise around the Curraun Peninsula. The narrow road passes an odd fortified tower and as it hugs the isolated southern edge the views across Clew Bay and out to sea are simply stunning.

After you cross the bridge onto Achill, cut left again on leaving Achill Sound, to pick up the Atlantic Drive, signed Wild Atlantic Way. It follows the island's remote southern shore, passing through the little fishing hamlet of **Dooega**, with its sheltered beach.

★ Keem Bay Beach BEACH
(🅿) Tucked away at the far west of the island, Keem Bay is Achill's most remote Blue Flag beach. The crescent of golden sands sits at the foot of steep cliffs, hemmed in by rock on three sides. Spiralling down to this perfect cove feels like finding the pot of gold at the end of an Irish rainbow. Beautiful.

It's a stunning drive here from Keel, 8km to the east, taking in expansive views across the water as the road climbs beside steep cliffs.

Achill Island

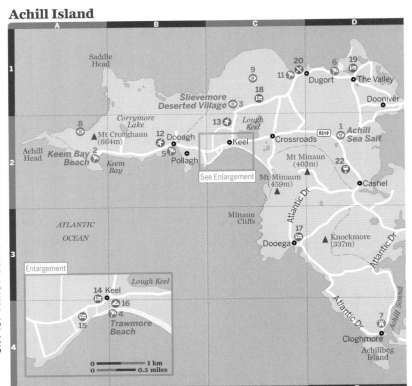

★ **Trawmore Beach**   BEACH
(Keel) Running 3km southeast from Keel, beautiful, Blue Flag, golden-sand Trawmore is among Achill's most photographed beaches. Be aware that there are dangerous rips from its centre to the eastern end (under the Minaun Cliffs). If you're swimming, heed the signs and stick to the western half.

★ **Slievemore**
Deserted Village   HISTORIC SITE
See p29.

★ **Achill Sea Salt**   VISITOR CENTRE
(☑ 098-47856; www.achillislandseasalt.ie; Bunacurry; adult/child €7/free; ☉ tours noon Thu & Fri) At the O'Malley's factory, tours reveal just how the family magics Achill's mineral-rich waters into flavoursome flakes of crunchy salt. After seeing demos on the crystallisation of brine and sampling regular and smoked versions on cherry tomatoes, it will be hard to resist a quick purchase in the on-site shop. Booking essential.

Grace O'Malley's Castle   CASTLE
(Kildownet Tower; Kildownet; ☉ dawn-dusk) FREE
The 40ft-high, 15th-century tower house rising beside the shore at Kildownet is associated with the pirate queen Grace O'Malley. Entering through a steel turnstile is an eerie experience – it reveals a tall hollow shell with slits for windows and a square hole in the roof.

Don Allum Monument   MONUMENT
(Dooagh) FREE In the village of Dooagh's main car park sits a slender, inscribed stone noting the epic achievement of Don Allum, the first person to row across the Atlantic Ocean in both directions. He landed here in September 1987 after 77 days at sea. He made the entire journey in a 6m-long, open plywood boat, dubbed the *QE3*, which had no satellite navigation or communication

Achill Island

◉ Top Sights

◉ Sights

⊕ Activities, Courses & Tours

⊜ Sleeping

⊗ Eating

◐ Drinking & Nightlife

systems. Opposite the monument, **Lourdie's bar** (The Pub; ☑ 098-43109; Dooagh; ⊙ 12.30pm-12.30am Mon-Sat, to 11.30pm Sun) has associated memorabilia.

Mulranny   VILLAGE

Rising from a narrow isthmus, the hillside village of Mulranny overlooks a wide Blue Flag beach on the road from Newport to Achill Sound and on the cusp of the Curraun Peninsula. It's a prime vantage point for counting the 365 or so seemingly saucer-sized islands that grace Clew Bay.

🏃 Activities

Achill Island is a wonderful place for walking and the views are terrific. Ramblers can climb **Mt Slievemore** (671m) or take on the longer climb of **Mt Croaghaun** (664m), Achill Head and a walk atop what locals claim are Europe's highest sea cliffs. There's also a good 4.3km loop starting at the beach

in Dooagh in the south. Achill Tourism (p85) produces 14 excellent downloadable guides to walks around the island.

Achill has many additional scalloped bays tame enough for swimming, including the Blue Flag beaches at Keem Bay (p81), **Dooega**, **Silver Strand** and **Golden Strand** – find the last two at Dugort in the north. Except in the height of the holiday season, these beaches are often deserted.

Pure Magic Achill Island (p84) runs lessons in kite-surfing and stand-up paddleboarding. It also does SUP rental.

Achill Bikes   CYCLING

(☑ 087 243 7686; www.achillbikes.com; Dooagh; adult/child rental per day from €20/14) Rents out a variety of bikes, including electric ones, per day for €50. Also offers advice on routes. Weekly rates are also available.

Calvey's Equestrian Centre　HORSE RIDING
(☑ 087 988 1093; www.calveysofachill.com; Slievemore; adult/child per 1½hr from €50/60) Calvey's arranges a wide variety of lessons, including taster sessions for novices, a four-day summer camp (€140) and, for experienced riders, a two-hour gallop (adult/child €60/70) on the sand.

Festivals & Events

Achill Island hosts several festivals during the year, including ones devoted to traditional Irish music, cycling, painting, boating and more. See www.achilltourism.com for the latest.

Scoil Acla Festival　CULTURAL
(☑ 085 881 9548; www.scoilacla.ie; ⊘ late Jul–early Aug) Traditional Irish music resonates for a week during this festival, which also has Irish dancing, culture and music workshops.

🛏 Sleeping

Achill's B&Bs are scattered along the main road from the bridge all the way to Keel, and you'll also find places to stay dotted along the shores.

★ Valley House　HOSTEL €
(☑ 085 216 7688; www.valley-house.com; The Valley; campsites per 2 people €21, dm/d €20/50; @ 🛜) Amid unruly gardens, this remote 32-bed hostel in a creaking old mansion has atmosphere to spare. JM Synge based his play *The Playboy of the Western World* on misadventures here and the subsequent film *Love and Rage* (1999) was also partially shot here.

Bonuses include scones for breakfast and a pub with patio tables. Breakfast for campers is another €5.

Keel Sandybanks Caravan & Camping Park　CAMPGROUND €
(☑ 098-43211; www.achillcamping.com; Keel; campsites per 2 adults €17-22, caravan per 2 nights from €195; ⊘ mid-Apr–Sep; 🛜) There are views of Keel beach from this campground, just a short stroll from town. If you're not keen on canvas, you can kip in a four-person caravan, which comes complete with bathrooms and TVs.

★ Pure Magic Achill Island　GUESTHOUSE €€
(☑ 085 243 9782; www.puremagic.ie; Slievemore Rd; s/d/f from €60/80/120; 🛜) There's a fun vibe at this lively 10-room spot near Dugort thanks to a buzzing bar and cafe with excellent pizza. Bedroom themes range from Moroccan and Brazilian to French, and you

can arrange lessons in kite-surfing (per three hours €130) and stand-up paddleboarding (per hour €40) and rent out stand-up paddleboards (per hour €15).

Achill Cliff House Hotel & Restaurant　GUESTHOUSE €€
(☑ 098-43400; www.achillcliff.com; Keel; d €120-150; 🛜) Sweeping views out to sea – even from the breakfast room – make this family-run guesthouse a great retreat. Furnishings are smart but comfy and the restaurant (mains €19 to €25) delivers superb fresh local seafood and creative takes on Irish classics.

Bervie　B&B €€
(☑ 098-43114; www.bervie-guesthouse-achill.com; Keel; s €80, d €110-150, f €165-225; 🛜) Former coastguard station Bervie occupies a spot plumb on the shore. It's a friendly place with 14 bright and cosy rooms, many with ocean views, and direct access to the beach from its well-tended garden. A playroom with a pool table chips in for wet days. Lauded evening meals are available on request.

🍴 Eating & Drinking

Cottage　CAFE €
(☑ 098-43966; Dugort; mains €6-17; ⊘ 10am-6pm Jun-Sep; ☑) The perfect pause to soak up the charms of the little seaside village of Dugort, the Cottage offers fab coffees and baked goods plus a tasty variety of sandwiches, seafood, and vegetarian and vegan specials. Relax outside at a picnic table with views.

★ Chalet　SEAFOOD €€
(☑ 087 230 7893; www.keembayfishproducts.ie; Keel; mains €17-30; ⊘ 6-10pm summer, shorter hours rest of year) The proprietors of Keem Bay Fish Products have been serving up their acclaimed smoked local salmon and other delicacies at this restaurant for decades. The menu changes with what's fresh, but expect a meal of the very best seafood.

Mickey's Bar　SEAFOOD €€
(☑ 098-45116; www.lavellesseasidehouse.com; Dooega; mains €9-15; ⊘ food served 6-8pm May-Sep) Friendly village pub Mickey's draws the locals for gossip, the occasional sing-a-long and simple but excellent seafood: smoked salmon, mussels and crab claws.

Lynott's　PUB
(☑ 086 084 3137; R319, Cashel; ⊘ hours vary) This tiny, traditional thatched roadside pub with flagstone floors and ancient benches is the real deal. There's no TV or radio or

even a hint of a ham-and-cheese toastie, just plenty of craic; music sessions are held here on Fridays at 10pm.

It's set back from the road and easy to miss: look for the sign with a finger pointing left off the R319 as you exit the village of Cashel, heading west.

ⓘ Information

There's an ATM in the village of Achill Sound. There are post offices in Keel and Achill Sound.

Achill Tourism (📞 098-20400; www.achilltourism.com; Davitt Quarter, Achill Sound; ⓧ 9am-5.30pm Mon-Fri, to 4pm Sat) Offers good walking and cycling information and a wealth of tips on island life.

Ballycastle & Around

POP 219

The main draw of the beautifully sited village of Ballycastle, consisting of a sole sloping street, is its megalithic tombs – one of the greatest concentrations in Europe – and some gorgeous coastal scenery, including one of Ireland's top photogenic experiences: the raw, isolated sea stack of Dun Briste at Downpatrick Head.

★ **Céide Fields**   ARCHAEOLOGICAL SITE
(📞 096-43325; www.heritageireland.ie; off R314; adult/child €5/3; ⓧ visitor centre 10am-6pm Jun-Sep, to 5pm Easter-May & Oct, last tour 1hr before closing) An exposed hillside 8km northwest of Ballycastle is home to one of the world's most extensive Stone Age monuments. So far stone-walled fields, houses and megalithic tombs – about half a million tonnes of stone – have been found, the legacy of a farming community nearly 6000 years old. The **visitor centre**, in a glass pyramid overlooking the site, gives a fascinating glimpse into these times. Be sure to take a **guided tour** of the site to fully appreciate the findings.

It was only during the 1930s that a local, Patrick Caulfield, was digging in the bog when he noticed a lot of piled-up stones buried beneath it. A full realisation of what lay under the sod didn't happen for another four decades, when his son Seamus began exploration of the area. Excavations are ongoing.

★ **Stella Maris**   HOTEL €€€
(📞 096-43322; www.stellamarisireland.com; Killerduff; r €155-195; ⓧ Easter-Oct; 🛜) With a turret at each end and a long glass-fronted veranda in between, Stella Maris is a charismatic sight. Dating from 1853, it was originally a British Coast Guard station, and later a convent. Today, upmarket rooms combine antiques, stylish modern furnishings and killer views of a lonely stretch of coast. Stella Maris is 2.5km northwest of Ballycastle

Mary's Cottage Kitchen   CAFE €
(📞 096-43361; Main St; snacks from €4; ⓧ 10am-5pm Wed-Sun) Mary makes everyone feel welcome at this charming place with good coffee, fresh-baked goods, lunch items, chocolate treats and a back garden, where campers have been known to overnight.

Killala & Around

POP 562

It's claimed that the ever-busy St Patrick founded Killala, and the Church of Ireland church sits on the site of the first Christian church in Ireland. The most noticeable sight, though, is the town's 25m-high round tower, which soars over Killala's heart.

★ **Lackan Strand**   BEACH
Lackan Bay's beach is a stunning and vast expanse of golden sand – it's particularly beautiful as the sun goes down, making it one of Ireland's most gorgeous bays. There's good surf here and plenty of places to get lost. Follow the R314 about 4.5km northwest from Killala, then turn at the signpost for Kilcummin.

★ **St Mary's Well**   RELIGIOUS SITE
(Tobar Mhuire; off R314; ⓧ 24hr) St Mary's is one of Ireland's most transfixing holy wells. An apparition of the Virgin Mary has drawn

---

WORTH A TRIP

DOWNPATRICK HEAD DETOUR

For a spectacular short looping detour off the main road (R314) to Killala, take the coast road north out of Ballycastle, passing **Downpatrick Head**, where you can view one of Mayo's most amazing sights, the sea stack of **Dun Briste** (www.dunbriste.com). Here is some of Mayo's most dramatic shoreline, with no end to the excitement. Look for the narrow lane to the head that takes you right up to the surf. Continue east and south, with **Lackan Bay** on your left until you rejoin the R314.

If driving west from Killala, look for the turn to Kilcummin 4.5km northwest of town and do the route in reverse.

Dun Briste (p85), Downpatrick Head
JOHANNES RIGG/SHUTTERSTOCK ©

begins in the car park of the parish church at Lackan Strand.

An optional 3km extension includes sweeping views of the region. Both trails are marked by fingerpost signs.

Ballina

POP 10,171

In addition to its excellent museum, Ballina is very much worth a visit to explore, spend the night at, or dine in the astonishing Belleek Castle.

◉ Sights

Belleek Castle　　　　　　　　CASTLE
(☏096-22400; www.belleekcastle.com; Castle Rd; adult/child €10/7.50; ⊙tours 11am, 2pm & 4pm)
Take a fascinating tour of this restored castle, built between 1825 and 1831 on the site of a medieval abbey. The castle was bought in the 1960s by fossil collector Marshall Doran, who gave it an eclectic and eccentric interior, some of it nautical (including the Spanish Armada bar). The tour also visits the Banquet Hall and Marshall Doran's collection of fossils, weaponry and armour. En route you will also encounter the last wolf shot in Connaught.

Jackie Clarke Collection　　　　MUSEUM
(☏096-73508; www.clarkecollection.ie; Pearse St; ⊙10am-5pm Tue-Sat) **FREE** Starting when he was 12 in 1939, the late Jackie Clarke was a businessman who amassed an extraordinary collection of 100,000 items covering 400 years of Irish history. With a lovely walled garden and housed in an 1881 bank building, this well-curated museum brims with eclectic surprises.

🏃 Activities

Salmon fishing is the main draw in Ballina, so most activities centre on angling on the River Moy. A list of fisheries and permit contacts is available at the tourist office. The season is February to September, but the best salmon fishing is June to August.

Ridge Pool Tackle Shop　　　　FISHING
(☏086 875 3648; Emmet St; ⊙9am-5pm Mon-Sat)
Information, supplies and licences are available at Ridge Pool Tackle Shop. Fly-casting lessons can also be arranged. The best fishing season is June to August.

🎊 Festivals & Events

Ballina Salmon Festival　　　　CULTURAL
See p30.

pilgrims here for centuries, and today a tumbledown 18th-century chapel covers the spot. A large thorn tree, garlanded with rosary beads and crucifixes, sprouts from the roof; inside, waters spill from an old stone vault, overseen by a statue of the Virgin.

St Mary's Well is a signed 1km walk from the approach road to Rosserk Abbey, off the R314.

Round Tower　　　　　　　　TOWER
Right at the centre of things and at the heart of Killala, the town's gorgeous 12th-century limestone round tower is perfectly preserved, although it was struck by lightning in the 19th century and repaired.

Rosserk Abbey　　　HISTORIC BUILDING
(off R314; ⊙dawn-dusk) Dipping its toes into the River Rosserk, this sublime Franciscan abbey dates from the mid-15th century. An eye-catching double piscina (perforated stone basin) is in the chancel: look for the exquisite carvings of a 2ft-high round tower (very rare to see one carved in this way) and two angels on either side of a Gothic arch.

The abbey is 4km south of Killala off the R314. Look for the signposts and then follow narrow farming lanes for another 5km.

Lackan Trail　　　　　　　WALKING
(www.mayowalks.ie; Lackan Church car park)
Follow beautiful Lackan Bay and discover ancient ring forts and megalithic tombs on this moderate and looping 8km walk that

🛏 Sleeping & Eating

Belleek Park   CAMPGROUND €
(📞096-71533; www.belleekpark.com; off R314;
campsites per adult €11; 🅿🛜) Landscaped
parkland, spacious pitches and a wealth of
facilities, including tennis courts, football
areas and a games room, make this campground some 3km north of Ballina popular
with families.

The three-person log cabins (per week
€350 to €600) come complete with bathroom, kitchen and bed linen.

★Belleek Castle   HOTEL €€€
(📞096-22400; www.belleekcastle.com; Castle Rd;
r €200-250; 🛜) Your chance to kip in a castle – imposing Belleek is eclectically decorated in ornate period style, with plush
rooms successfully pairing four-poster beds
with flat-screen TVs. This dollop of luxury is
permeated with a gorgeous sense of seclu-
sion and is set in vast grounds by the River
Moy. Breakfast included.

It's also a fine place for dinner in the
Library Restaurant (📞096-22400; www.
belleekcastle.com; Belleek Castle; mains €28-34,
8 courses €73; ⊙2.30-9pm) , while fascinating
tours are run throughout the day for visitors.

**★Mount Falcon
Country House Hotel**   LUXURY HOTEL €€€
(📞096-74472; www.mountfalcon.com; Foxford Rd;
r from €180; 🛜🏊) Hidden away on 40 hectares between Lough Conn and the River
Moy lies this stunning place to stay. Rooms
in the gorgeous 1870s mansion ooze old-
world grandeur, while those in the modern
extension have a more contemporary edge.
Anglers will be hooked by the exclusive fish-
ery, while the tranquil tempo is endlessly
relaxing. Find it 5km south of Ballina.

Special offers reduce prices to around
€150 per night.

Ice House Hotel   BOUTIQUE HOTEL €€€
(📞096-23500; www.icehousehotel.ie; The Quay;
r €125-307; 🛜) Up-close views of the serene
River Moy estuary are the main draw at this
32-room hotel that combines an elegant
restored namesake heritage building with a
pared-down, modern wing and a spa, right
by the water. It's 2km northeast of the centre
and close to good waterfront pubs.

★Clarke's Seafood Delicatessen   DELI €
(📞096-21022; www.clarkes.ie; O'Rahilly St; treats
from €5; ⊙9am-6pm Mon-Sat) Couldn't catch
a salmon? The wizards at award-winning

Clarke's will sell you their house oak-smoked
salmon in myriad forms, plus all manner of
other picnic-friendly fishy creations. If you
have caught your own fish, they'll smoke it
for you too.

ℹ Information

The **tourist office** (📞096-72800; www.north
mayo.ie; 44 Lower Pearse St; ⊙10am-5pm Mon-
Sat, closed Sat Oct-Apr) is in the centre of town,
opposite the Jackie Clarke Collection museum.

Castlebar & Around
POP 12,068

Mayo's county town, Castlebar, is a traffic-
thronged hub of shops and services, but
there are useful facilities and some good
hotels, and its proximity to some big sights
makes it a handy short-term base. Most
places of interest lie outside the town centre.

◉ Sights

**★National Museum
of Country Life**   MUSEUM
(📞094-903 1755; www.museum.ie; off N5, Turlough Park; ⊙10am-5pm Tue-Sat, 1-5pm Sun &
Mon) 🆓 The extensive and engrossing
displays of this riverside museum delve
into Ireland's fascinating rural traditions
and skills. It's set in a modern, photogenic facility that overlooks a lake in the
lush grounds of 19th-century **Turlough
Manor.** A branch of the National Museum
of Ireland, the museum explores everything
from the role of the potato to boat building,
herbal cures and traditional clothes. It has
a good cafe and a shop; it's 8km northeast
of Castlebar.

The lovely **Turlough Round Tower** is visible from the grounds.

★Ballintubber Abbey   CATHEDRAL
(📞094-903 0934; www.ballintubberabbey.ie;
Ballintubber; donation requested; ⊙9am-midnight,
tours 9.30am-5pm Mon-Fri, by arrangement Sat &
Sun) 🆓 Imposing Ballintubber Abbey is
the only church in Ireland founded by an
Irish king that remains in use. It's reputed
to have been established in 1216 next to
the site of an earlier church founded by
St Patrick after he came down from Croagh Patrick. Its history is tumultuous: the
abbey was burned by Normans, seized by
James I and suppressed by Henry VIII.
It's signposted off the N84, 13km south of
Castlebar.

★ Moore Hall   HISTORIC BUILDING

(☎ 098-25293; www.moorehall.net; Lough Carra; ☉ dawn-dusk) **FREE** With towering walls engulfed in ivy and empty windows, Moore Hall is an astonishing and atmospheric ruin. Set beside Lough Carra, it was built in the 1790s and burned down in 1923 during the Civil War, its priceless library of old books and splendid panelling going up in flames. The surrounding woodland is a joy to explore. You can also wander around the totally overgrown walled garden, which may, along with the house, be eventually restored.

✕ Eating

★ Rua Deli & Cafe   IRISH €

(☎ 094-928 6072; www.caferua.com; Spencer St; mains €9-12; ☉ 8.30am-6pm Mon-Sat; 🖪) Artisan, organic, local food packs the shelves and tables of this gourmet deli-cafe. Picnic goodies include Carrowholly cheese, Ballina smoked salmon and luscious salads. Upstairs, amid artfully mismatched furniture, Mayo produce is teamed with global flavours such as harrisa, pesto and toasted seeds.

COUNTY SLIGO

County Sligo packs as much poetry, myth and folklore into its countryside's lush splendour as any shamrock lover and archaeologist could hope for. It was Sligo that most inspired the Nobel laureate, poet and dramatist William Butler Yeats (1865–1939). Ever fascinated by Irish mysticism, he was intrigued by places such as prehistoric Carrowmore Megalithic Cemetery, Knocknarea Cairn, iconic and hulking Benbulben and cute little Innisfree Island.

And it's no complacent backwater: there's a vibrant and creative food culture, and the coast's surf is internationally renowned.

Sligo Town

POP 19,199

Sligo Town makes a fantastic, low-key and easily manageable base for exploring Yeats country, and the countryside out of town is gorgeous.

⊙ Sights

★ Model   GALLERY

(☎ 071-914 1405; www.themodel.ie; The Mall; admission varies; ☉ 10am-5pm Tue-Sat, 10.30am-3.30pm Sun) The Model houses an impressive collection of contemporary Irish art including works by Jack B Yeats (WB's brother and one of Ireland's most important modern artists) and Louis le Brocquy.

Sligo Abbey   HISTORIC BUILDING

(☎ 071-914 6406; www.heritageireland.ie; Abbey St; adult/child €5/3; ☉ 10am-6pm Apr-Oct) This handsome Dominican friary was built around 1252 but burned down in the 15th century, to be later rebuilt. Friends in high places saved the abbey from the worst ravages of the Elizabethan era, and rescued the sole sculpted altar to survive the Reformation. The doorways reach only a few feet high at the abbey's rear; the ground around it was swollen by the mass graves from years of famine and war.

Yeats Memorial Building   MUSEUM

(☎ 071-914 2693; www.yeatssociety.com; Hyde Bridge; €3; ☉ 10am-5pm Mon-Fri) In a pretty setting in a former 1895 bank, the **WB Yeats Exhibition** has details of his life, draft manuscripts and special summer programs. Admission includes a tour of the collection.

Sligo County Museum   MUSEUM

See p32.

Michael Quirke's Studio   STATUE

(☎ 071-914 2624; Wine St; ☉ 9.30am-12.30pm & 3-5.30pm Mon-Sat) **FREE** Don't miss a chat with woodcarver, raconteur and local legend Michael Quirke as he hand-carves his wooden creations. Opening times can vary, so take a look at what's on display in the window if he's popped out.

🏃 Activities

★ Sea Trails   WALKING

(☎ 087 240 5071; www.seatrails.ie; walks from €20) Led by the resourceful and knowledgeable Auriel, this highly recommended company runs interesting walks concentrating on Yeats, ancient features and natural beauty in and near the coast, including Armada sights and the stunning local geology. She also runs heritage horseback tours (adult/child €60/40), which are suitable for beginners.

Chain Driven Cycles   CYCLING

(☎ 071-912 9008; www.chaindrivencycles.com; 23 High St; per day/week from €15/45; ☉ 10am-6pm Tue-Fri, to 5pm Sat, noon-6pm Mon) Offers hybrid-, electric- and road-bike hire. Rates include helmet.

✨ Festivals & Events

Tread Softly   CULTURAL
(www.treadsoftly.ie; ⊙ late Jul) Poetry, music, drama and art characterise this 10-day celebration of the life and work of WB Yeats.

**Yeats International
Summer School**   LITERATURE
(www.yeatssociety.com; ⊙ Jul-Aug) Now into its sixth decade, this prestigious 10-day festival brings lectures, workshops, drama, readings and walking tours to Sligo town.

Sligo Live   CULTURAL
(www.sligolive.ie; ⊙ late Oct) Sligo's biggest cultural event is this live-music festival over five days in autumn.

🛏 Sleeping

Railway Hostel   HOSTEL €
(☑ 087 690 5539; www.therailway.ie; 1 Union Pl; dm/s/tw from €20/27/46; P 🛜) Great rates, a clutch of parking spaces and cosy dorms – many featuring single beds as well as bunk beds – sit inside this cheery hostel, where the train-themed decor meshes with the name. A basic breakfast of tea, coffee and cereal is included in the price.

★ Glass House   HOTEL €€
(☑ 071-919 4300; www.theglasshouse.ie; Swan Point; s €103, d €112-129, ste €138-155; 🛜) You can't miss this cool and contemporary four-star hotel in the centre of town, its sharp glass facade jutting skyward. Inside, the food areas have good river views, there are two bars and the 116 well-equipped rooms come in a choice of zesty colours.

Clayton Hotel   HOTEL €€
(☑ 071-911 9000; www.claytonhotelsligo.com; Clarion Rd; d/f from €115/125; 🧳 ⊠) Looking vaguely reminiscent of a Harry Potter film set, the huge, historic, grey-stone Clayton bristles with Hogwarts-esque turrets, gables and mini-spires. The rooms are massive, as are the grounds; you'll also find a swimming pool, spa and loads of facilities for kids.

A wealth of room-only, early-booking deals can bring prices down.

Sligo Park Hotel   HOTEL €€
(☑ 071-919 0400; www.sligoparkhotel.com; Pearse Rd; s/d/f from €110/120/145; P 🛜 ⊠) Landscaped grounds, mature trees, and an array of facilities help lend this modern hotel a country-club air. The pretty, tastefully decorated rooms are bright and modern. It's 3km south of town.

YEATS COUNTRY

County Sligo's lush hills, ancient monuments and simple country life inspired Nobel laureate, poet and dramatist William Butler Yeats (1865–1939) from an early age. Despite living almost all his life abroad, Yeats returned here frequently, enamoured of the lakes, the looming hulk of Benbulben and the idyllic pastoral setting.

An Crúiscin Lan   GUESTHOUSE €€
(☑ 087 233 1573; www.bandbsligo.ie; Connolly St; s/d €50/85; P 🛜) A friendly welcome, fair-sized rooms, good location and parking all add to the appeal at this convivial B&B, as do the porridge and Irish fry-ups for breakfast. Some rooms share bathrooms.

🍴 Eating

★ Fabio's   ICE CREAM €
(☑ 087 177 2732; Wine St; treats from €2.50; ⊙ 11am-6pm Mon-Thu, to 6.30pm Fri & Sat, noon-6pm Sun) Local hero Fabio makes arguably Ireland's best Italian gelato and sorbets from mostly local and natural ingredients. The frequently changing flavour offer is remarkable: from white chocolate and pistachio crunch to raspberry lime sorbet. In summer he's often open till 7pm.

★ Lyons Cafe   IRISH €
(☑ 071-914 2969; www.lyonscafe.com; Quay St; mains €8-16; ⊙ 9am-6pm Mon-Sat) The cafe in Sligo's flagship department store, Lyons, first opened in 1926, but the food served in the airy, 1st-floor eatery is bang up to date. Acclaimed chef and cookbook author Gary Stafford offers a fresh and seasonal menu that's inventive yet casual.

Kate's Kitchen   CAFE €
(☑ 071-914 3022; www.kateskitchen.ie; 3 Castle St; mains from €7; ⊙ 8.30am-5.30pm Mon-Sat) Only the best local foodstuffs are served at this welcoming, contemporary cafe-store. All the ingredients for a prime picnic are there along with prepared foods. The tiny cafe is a cheery spot for punchy coffee and homemade lunch.

★ Hargadons   PUB FOOD €€
(☑ 071-915 3709; www.hargadons.com; 4/5 O'Connell St; mains €10-25; ⊙ food noon-3.30pm & 4-9pm Mon-Sat) You'll have a hard time leaving this superb 1868 inn with its winning blend of old-world fittings and gastropub

Sligo Town

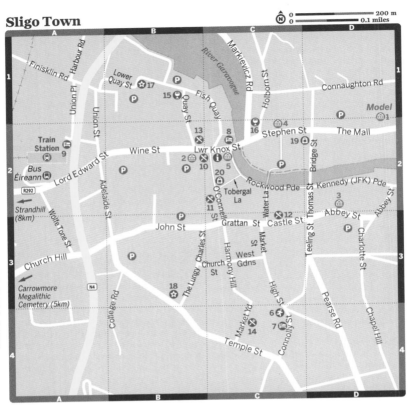

Sligo Town

style. The uneven floors, peat fire, antique signage, snug corners and bowed shelves laden down with ancient bottles lend it a wonderful charm. The great-value food is renowned, transforming local ingredients such as oysters with continental flair.

Montmartre   FRENCH €€
(☑071-916 9901; www.montmartrerestaurant.ie; 1 Market Yard; mains €17-26; ⊙5-11pm Tue-Sat) Tucked away on a back road by the market sits an excellent French restaurant serving unpretentious but top-quality food. The menu spotlights local meats, but seafood lovers are well catered for too. Book ahead.

The 'smart eater' menu, available all evening Tuesday to Thursday, and 6pm to 7pm on Friday and Saturday, is excellent value (two/three courses €22/27).

🍷 Drinking & Entertainment

Harp Tavern   PUB
(☑071-914 2473; Quay St; ⊙noon-11.30pm Sun-Thu, to 1am Fri & Sat) This all-around good pub has a glowing stove, a genuinely welcoming vibe, good bar food and live music on Friday, Saturday and Sunday nights. See the Facebook page for updates on upcoming gigs.

Thomas Connolly   PUB
(☑071-919 4920; www.thomasconnollysligo.com; Markievicz Rd & Holborn St; ⊙11am-11.30pm Sun-Thu, to 12.30pm Fri & Sat) Join the locals amid the faded photos, mottled mirrors, craft beer and live music ranging from trad to jazz at this magnificent historic pub.

Blue Raincoat Theatre Company   THEATRE
(☑071-917 0431; www.blueraincoat.com; Lower Quay St) A former abattoir is home to innovative theatre company Blue Raincoat, whose program includes original productions plus Yeats in the summer.

Hawk's Well Theatre   THEATRE
(☑071-916 1518; www.hawkswell.com; Temple St) This well-regarded 340-seat theatre presents concerts, dance and drama for children and adults.

🛍 Shopping

★**Liber**   BOOKS
(☑071-914 2219; www.liber.ie; 35 O'Connell St; ⊙9am-6pm Mon-Sat) The section on local literary legend WB Yeats at this fabulous bookshop is extensive; staff are also happy to advise on books about County Sligo's history and other local authors. There's an eclectic range of music CDs and vinyl too.

Bookmart   BOOKS
(www.bookmart.ie; 6 Bridge St; ⊙10am-6pm Mon-Sat) A treasure trove of titles, from duffed-up Asimov to Dylan Thomas, and Sylvia Plath to Primo Levi, share space on stuffed shelves

in Bookmart, overseen by friendly, helpful staff.

Look out for poetry readings too (8pm on the first Thursday of the month), and other cultural events.

ℹ Information

The **tourist office** (☑071-916 1201; www.sligo tourism.ie; cnr O'Connell & Wine Sts; ⊙9am-5pm Mon-Fri, 9.30am-5pm Sat, closed Sat Nov-Apr) has information on the whole northwest region, plus good walking info and loads of maps and literature. In August the office also opens on Sunday (10am to 2pm).

Lough Gill & Around

Beautiful, mirror-like Lough Gill (Lake of Brightness) was a place of great inspiration for Yeats. The lake, which is dotted with some 20 small islands, is a mere 8km southeast of Sligo town and simple to reach. It's shaded by two magical swaths of woodland – Hazelwood and Slish Wood – which have waymarked trails; there are good views of Innisfree Island from the latter.

You can take a cruise on the lake from atmospheric **Parke's Castle** (☑071-916 4149; www.heritageireland.ie; off R286, Kilmore; adult/child €5/3; ⊙10am-6pm Easter-Sep), in nearby County Leitrim. Watch for the shadows of huge salmon and the ripples of otters.

The lake is immediately southeast of Sligo town. Take the R286 along the north shore for the most interesting views. The southern route on the R287 is less interesting until you reach **Dooney Rock**. Immortalised by Yeats in 'The Fiddler of Dooney' (1899), this fissured limestone knoll bulges awkwardly upward by the lough's southern shore. There's a great lake view from the top and you can park right at the bottom. Photographs over the lake can be stunning as the sun sinks at the end of the day. It's 7km southeast of Sligo town on the R287.

Pint-sized **Innisfree Island** lies tantalisingly close to the lough's southeastern shore, but, alas, can't be accessed. Still, it's visible from the shore. Its air of tranquillity so moved Yeats that he famously wrote 'The Lake Isle of Innisfree' (1890) about it. Access the best vantage point of the island from a small road that starts at the junction of the R287 and the R290. Follow the winding lane for 4.2km to a small parking area by the water.

County Clare

County Clare combines spectacular windswept landscapes and vibrant Irish culture. The ocean relentlessly pounds Clare's coast year-round, eroding rock into fantastic formations, and fashioning sheer rock crags. Right along the coast, the waves are a magnet for surfers, and surf schools set up on many of Clare's beaches in summer.

ENNIS

POP 25,276

Today formal sights are few, but the town centre, with its narrow, pedestrian-friendly streets, is enjoyable to wander. Handily situated 23km north of Shannon Airport, it makes an ideal base for exploring the county: you can reach any part of Clare in under two hours from here.

◉ Sights & Activities

★ **Ennis Friary**   CHURCH
(☑ 065-682 9100; www.heritageireland.ie; Abbey St; adult/child €5/3; ⊘ 10am-6pm Easter-Sep, to 5pm Oct) North of the Square, Ennis Friary was founded by Donnchadh Cairbreach O'Brien, a king of Thomond, between 1240 and 1249. A mix of structures dating between the 13th and 19th centuries, the friary has a graceful five-section window dating from the late 13th century, a McMahon tomb (1460) with alabaster panels depicting scenes from the Passion, and a particularly fine *Ecce Homo* panel portraying a stripped and bound Christ.

Clare Museum   MUSEUM
(☑ 065-682 3382; www.clarelibrary.ie; Arthur's Row; ⊘ 9.30am-1pm & 2-5.30pm Mon-Sat Jun-Sep, Tue-Sat Oct-May) FREE At this diverting little museum, the 'Riches of Clare' exhibition

tells the story of Clare from 8000 years ago to the present day using authentic artefacts grouped into five themes: earth (geology, seasons and agriculture), power (such as hill forts and tower houses), faith (Christianity's influence), water (the county's relationship with the River Shannon and the Atlantic) and energy (particularly Clare's musical and sporting prowess).

Daniel O'Connell Monument   MONUMENT
(The Square) Set on a soaring column, a statue of Daniel O'Connell (aka the 'Great Liberator') presides over the Square.

O'Connell's election to the British parliament by a huge majority in 1828 forced Britain to lift its ban on Catholic MPs and led to the Act of Catholic Emancipation a year later.

Ennis Cathedral   CATHEDRAL
(☑ 065-682 4043; www.ennisparish.com; O'Connell St; ⊘ 7.30am-8pm Mon-Fri, 9am-7pm Sat & Sun) FREE Consecrated in 1843, this impressive structure had its tower and spire added in 1874, and was elevated to the status of a cathedral in 1990. A highlight is its 1930-built organ.

Tierney's Cycles   CYCLING
(☑ 065-682 9433; www.clarebikehire.com; 17 Abbey St; bike rental per day/week from €24/85;

9.30am-6pm) Tierney's rents well-maintained road and racing bikes. Hire includes a lock and a repair kit.

Ennis Walking Tours
WALKING

(☑087 648 3714; www.enniswalkingtours.com; adult/child €10/5; ☉11am Mon, Tue & Thu-Sat May-Oct) Tales of famine, murder, riots and rebellion bring to life the story of Ennis' history on these excellent 75-minute walking tours, departing from the tourist office (p95) on Arthur's Row.

🎉 Festivals & Events

Fleadh Nua
CULTURAL

See p20.

Ennis Trad Festival
MUSIC

(www.ennistradfest.com; ☉early–mid-Nov) Traditional music in venues across town keeps the tunes flowing during November's five-day festival.

🛏 Sleeping

★ Rowan Tree Hostel
HOSTEL €

(☑065-686 8687; www.rowantreehostel.ie; Harmony Row; dm €25-29, d €79-89, f €125; 🛜) Balconies overlooking the swift-flowing River Fergus; bright, airy dorms; and doubles with Egyptian linen add to the appeal at this town-centre hostel. It's set in a grand 1740-built former gentlemen's club, and fantastic facilities include a kitchen, a laundry and the excellent Cafe Bar (p94) in the former ballroom.

Ardilaun Guesthouse
B&B €

(☑065-682 2311; purcells.ennis@eircom.net; Ballycoree; s/d €44/68; 🅿🛜) Drop a line into the River Fergus or just watch the sunset from the rear deck of this B&B around 3km north of the centre, off the R458. Pluses include an on-site fitness room and sauna, and friendly owners who can help arrange transport into town.

Temple Gate Hotel
HOTEL €€

(☑065-682 3300; www.templegatehotel.com; The Square; s/d/f from €131/131/191; 🅿🛜) The soaring cathedral-ceilinged lobby at this epicentral 70-room hotel was once part of the 19th-century Sisters of Mercy convent. Upper-floor rooms (reached by a lift) have views over Ennis' rooftops, but try to avoid ground-floor rooms facing the car park at the rear. There's an on-site restaurant and a great bar, the Preachers Pub, which also serves quality bar food.

★ Old Ground Hotel
HOTEL €€€

(☑065-682 8127; www.oldgroundhotelennis.com; O'Connell St; s €130, d €180-200, ste €230-275; 🛜) Entered through a lobby of polished floorboards, cornice-work, antiques and open fires, this prestigious landmark dates back to the 1800s. The 83 rooms vary greatly in size and decor, which ranges from historic to cutting-edge. Kids under 16 staying in their parents' room are charged €25 per night. The ground-floor Poet's Corner Bar (p19) is one of Ennis' best pubs.

🍴 Eating

Most of Ennis' pubs serve food, some of good quality; there are also some excellent delis and cafes.

The Ennis **farmers market** (www.ennisfarmersmarket.com; Roslevan Shopping Centre, Tulla Rd; ☉8am-2pm Fri) 🌱 is some 3km northeast of town and features prime produce, the vast majority of which comes from County Clare or within 30 miles of the market.

Food Heaven
CAFE €

(☑065-682 2722; www.food-heaven.ie; 21 Market St; dishes €6-12; ☉8.30am-6pm Mon-Sat; 🛜) The aptly named Food Heaven rustles up creative, fresh fare right from the American-style breakfast pancakes, via lunchtime open crayfish sandwiches through to afternoon teas. Be ready to queue at lunch for its renowned handmade sausage rolls.

Souper
CAFE €

(☑065-682 3901; 10 Merchant Sq; soups from €4.50; ☉9am-5pm Mon-Sat; 🌱) The choice of soups changes daily at this cosy cafe, which dishes up warming bowls of creamy garden pea, French onion with croutons, vegan leek and potato, and chicken and tarragon. Paninis, wraps and sandwiches fill any gaps.

Ennis Gourmet Store
DELI €

(☑065-684 3314; www.ennisgourmet.com; 1 Old Barrack St; dishes €8-16; ☉10am-8pm Mon-Wed, to 10pm Thu-Sat, noon-6pm Sun) Gourmet produce – from Burren smoked salmon and whiskey marmalade to fine French wines – fills the shelves of this delightful deli, which has a handful of seats inside and out. Simple but delicious dishes change daily but might include cauliflower soup, roast beetroot salad or warm mackerel on brioche.

Town Hall
IRISH €€

(☑065-682 8127; www.flynnhotels.com; O'Connell St; mains lunch €9-17, dinner €19-28; ☉10am-9.45pm Mon-Sat, to 9.30pm Sun; 🛜) At this smart

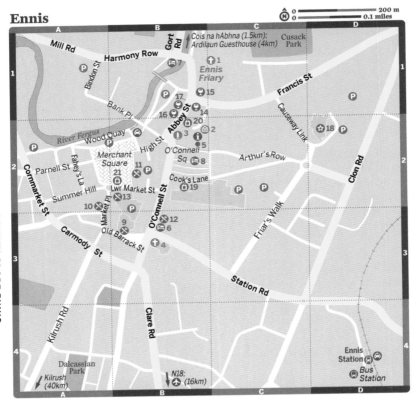

bistro attached to the neighbouring Old Ground Hotel (p93) local ingredients take centre stage: Clare lamb, Fergus Bay crab, Sixmilebridge free-range pork and Shannon Estuary monkfish. Scones, jam and coffee are served for afternoon tea, while candlelit tables create an intimate ambience at night.

Rowan Tree Cafe Bar   FUSION €€
(☑ 065-686 8669; www.rowantreecafebar.ie; Harmony Row; mains €8-14; ⊙ 10.30am-11pm; ☏☑☑🏠) A one-time ballroom, the dining room here has high ceilings, fairy lights and 18th-century wooden floors, while tables outside have river views. Global-themed dishes are packed with local, seasonal ingredients; treats include St Tola's goat-cheese fritters, west-coast crab linguini, and lamb and feta burgers. A cracking Sunday brunch draws the crowds.

The extensive children's menu features healthy options, with free mini-bowls of mash and soup for the under-twos.

Drinking & Entertainment

As the capital of a renowned music county, Ennis pulses with pubs featuring trad music a couple of times a week year-round and often nightly during summer. Custy's Music Shop is a great place to find out about live gigs; the tourist office also collates weekly listings.

Nora Culligans   PUB
(☑ 065-682 4954; www.noraculligans.com; Abbey St; ⊙ 4-11.30pm Mon-Thu, to 2am Fri, noon-2am Sat, noon-midnight Sun; ☏) Magnificently restored, cavernous Nora Culligans retains original features including the front bar's ornate two-storey-high whiskey cabinets and timber panelling in the back bar. It's an atmospheric venue for live music across a diverse array of genres, from jazz and blues to acoustic singer-songwriters and reggae as well as trad.

Brogan's   PUB
See p18.

Ennis

Poet's Corner Bar PUB
See p19.

Cois na hAbhna TRADITIONAL MUSIC
See p20.

Glór PERFORMING ARTS
(☑065-684 3103; www.glor.ie; Causeway Link; ☉box office 10am-5pm Mon-Sat) In a striking modern building, Clare's cultural centre hosts theatre, dance, traditional music, film, photography, art and more.

🔒 Shopping

★ **Scéal Eile Books** BOOKS
(☑065-684 8648; www.scealeilebooks.ie; 16 Lower Market St; ☉11am-6pm Mon-Sat) A delight to explore, this emerald-green-painted bookshop overflows with new and secondhand literature, including rare titles across all genres from poetry to sci-fi and travel. A stove at the rear, ensconced between two armchairs, creates a wonderfully cosy atmosphere. Book readings and cultural events regularly take place.

Custy's Music Shop MUSICAL INSTRUMENTS
(☑065-682 1727; www.custysmusic.com; Cook's Lane; ☉9am-6pm Mon-Sat) A must-stop shop for Irish music, with instruments, musical paraphernalia and a wealth of info about the local scene.

Ennis Bookshop BOOKS
(☑065-708 1300; www.ennisbookshop.ie; 13 Abbey St; ☉10am-6pm Mon-Sat) Independent Ennis Bookshop has a strong kids' section, general fiction and nonfiction, and a vast range of stationery.

ℹ Information

Ennis' **tourist office** (☑1850 230 330; www.visitennis.com; Arthur's Row; ☉9.30am-5.30pm Tue-Fri, 9am-5pm Sat) is housed in the same building as the Clare Museum.

ℹ Getting Around

There's a big car park southeast of the tourist office on Friar's Walk and one alongside the river just off Abbey St.

SOUTHWESTERN & WESTERN CLARE

Your best days in the county's west may be spent on the smallest roads you can find.

South of the plunging Cliffs of Moher to the beach resort of Kilkee, the land flattens, with vistas that sweep across pastures and dunes to the horizon. Some of Ireland's finest surf rolls in to shore near the low-key beach towns of Lahinch, Miltown Malbay and Doonbeg.

Kilkee is the main town of the Loop Head Peninsula. Beautiful and dramatic in equal measure, its soaring cliffs stretching to the lighthouse-crowned tip are major milestones on an already breathtaking shore.

Inland, don't miss the charming heritage town of Ennistimon and its surging cascades.

ℹ️ Getting There & Away

Shannon Ferry Limited (☑ 065-905 3124; www. shannonferries.com; cars €20, motorcyclists, cyclists & pedestrians €5; ⊘7am-9pm Mon-Sat, 9am-9pm Sun Jun-Aug, 7am-8pm Mon-Sat, 9am-8pm Sun Apr, May & Sep, 7am-7pm Mon-Sat, 9am-7pm Sun Oct-Mar) runs a ferry between Killimer in County Clare and **Tarbert** (☑ 068-905 3124; www.shannonferries.com; cars €20, motor-cyclists, cyclists & pedestrians €5; ⊘7.30am-8.30pm Mon-Sat, from 9.30am Sun Apr-Sep, longer hours Jun-Aug, shorter hours Oct-Mar; 📶) in County Kerry, departing hourly on the hour from Killimer and on the half-hour from Tarbert. Journey time is 20 minutes. It's a great shortcut, saving you 134km by road via Limerick.

Kilrush

POP 2719

The lively town of Kilrush (Cill Rois) has a strikingly wide main street that reflects its origins as a port and market town in the 19th century.

From the west coast's biggest marina at Kilrush Creek, ferries run 3km offshore to Scattery Island, home to magnificent early Christian ruins. Cruises also depart from the marina to view bottlenose dolphins living in the estuary, which is an important calving region for the mammals.

👁️ Sights & Activities

A 1.5km signposted walking trail, the **Dolphin Trail**, leads west from Kilrush's central square and is dotted with information panels, sculptures and murals.

★ Vandeleur Walled Garden   GARDENS
See p48.

Shannon Dolphin Centre   MUSEUM
(www.shannondolphins.ie; Merchants Quay; ⊘10am-6pm May–mid-Sep) FREE The 170-plus bottlenose dolphins swimming out in the Shannon are monitored by this dedicated research facility. In addition to learning about its latest work, you can listen to acoustic recordings and watch a 20-minute film about the playful cetaceans, a population unique to the area.

West Clare Railway   RAIL
(☑ 087 791 9289; www.westclarerailway.ie; N67; steam ticket adult/child €15/8, diesel €10/5; ⊘1-4pm May-Sep, days vary) A 2km vestige of the historic West Clare Railway line survives near Moyasta, 5km northwest of Kilrush. A beautiful steam-powered train was privately restored by Jackie Whelan, who now runs occasional Steam and Diesel Days, when the train shuttles back and forth over the open land. Call ahead for the schedule.

Dolphin Discovery   CRUISE
See p48.

🛏️ Sleeping & Eating

Kilrush has a hostel, pub accommodation and several B&Bs. There are also good options in Kilkee, 14km northwest.

Cafes are scattered throughout town; pubs also serve food.

Self-caterers will find supermarkets as well as a weekly **farmers' market** (Market Sq; ⊘9am-2pm Thu) 🥖 on the main square.

Katie O'Connor's Holiday Hostel   HOSTEL €
(☑ 065-905 1133; www.katieshostel.com; 50 Frances St; dm/d/tr from €22/40/50; ⊘mid-Mar–Oct; 📶) Dating from the 18th century, this tall townhouse once belonged to the powerful Vandeleur family. Today it's a well-equipped IHH-affiliated hostel with clean dorms and private rooms with bathrooms.

Potter's Hand   CAFE €
(☑ 065-905 2968; 3 Vandeleur St; dishes €3-8; ⊘9am-5pm Tue-Sat, to 4.30pm Mon; 🅿️♿) The Potter's Hand is the kind of calm, cool cafe you wish was on your own doorstep. Shelves stacked with books sit beside counters showcasing crumbly fruit scones and home-made treats: coffee and walnut, and plum and polenta cakes, and nutty protein balls.

Buttermarket Cafe   CAFE €
(☑ 065-905 1822; Burton St; mains €5-12; ⊘10am-4pm Mon-Thu, to 5pm Fri & Sat, 11am-4pm Sun; 📶) A courtyard that's a sun trap in fine weather might draw you here. Or that hot specials including stews and shepherd's pie, or drinks spanning salted caramel lattes, cinnamon hot chocolates, and mint-mocha frappuccinos.

Crotty's   PUB
(☑ 065-905 2470; www.crottyspubkilrush.com; Market Sq; ⊘9am-11.30pm Sun-Fri, to 12.30am Sat; 📶) Crotty's brims with character, thanks to an old-fashioned high bar, intricately tiled floors and a series of snugs decked out with retro furnishings. Trad sessions take place at 9.30pm on Tuesday and Wednesday year-round; less traditional bands play most weekends.

Crotty's serves basic pub fare (mains €10 to €22), and has five heritage-style guest rooms upstairs (doubles from €85).

SCATTERY ISLAND

The uninhabited, windswept and treeless **Scattery Island** (☎ 087 995 8427; www.heritage
ireland.ie; ⊗ visitor centre 10am-6pm late May-late Sep), in the estuary 3km southwest of
Kilrush, was the site of a Christian settlement founded by St Senan in the 6th century.
Its 36m-high round tower, the best preserved in Ireland, has its entrance at ground level
instead of the usual position high above the foundation. The evocative ruins of six medieval churches include the 9th-century **Cathedral of St Mary** (Teampall Naomh Mhuire) – part of **St Senan's Monastery**.

Also here are a **lighthouse** and an **artillery battery**, built during the Napoleonic
wars, at the southern end of the island. A free exhibition on the history and wildlife of the
Heritage Service–administered island is housed in the Scattery Island Visitor Centre.
The centre also provides free 45-minute tours to St Senan's Monastery.

Scattery Island Ferries (☎ 085 250 5512; www.scatteryislandtours.com; Kilrush Marina;
adult/child return €20/10; ⊗ late May-Aug) runs boats from Kilrush to the island; the journey takes 15 to 20 minutes. There's no strict timetable as the trips are subject to tidal
and weather conditions, but there are usually two sailings a day between June and September. Time spent on the island is usually between two and five hours. Buy tickets at
the small kiosk at **Kilrush Marina** (☎ 065-905 2072; www.kilrushmarina.ie; Kilrush Creek)
and bring a decent pair of walking shoes.

Loop Head Peninsula

A sliver of land between the Shannon Estuary and the pounding Atlantic, windblown
Loop Head Peninsula has an ends-of-the-
earth feel. As you approach along the R487,
sea begins to appear on both flanks as land
tapers to a narrow shelf. On a clear day, the
lighthouse-capped headland at Loop Head
(Ceann Léime), Clare's southernmost point,
has staggering views to counties Kerry and
Galway. The often-deserted wilds of the
head are perfect for exploration, but be extra
careful near the cliff edge.

On the northern side of the cliff near the
point, a dramatic crevice has been cleaved
into the coastal cliffs where you'll first hear
and then see a teeming bird-breeding area.
Guillemots, choughs and razorbills are
among the squawkers nesting in the rocky
niches.

A long hiking trail runs along the cliffs
to the peninsula's main town, Kilkee. A
handful of other tiny settlements dot the
peninsula.

The website www.loophead.ie is an excellent source of local information.

◉ Sights & Activities

Loop Head Lighthouse LIGHTHOUSE
(www.loophead.ie; Loop Head; adult/child
€5/2; ⊗ 10am-6pm mid-Mar–early Nov) On a
90m-high cliff, this 23m-tall working lighthouse, complete with a Fresnel lens, rises up
above Loop Head. Guided tours (included in
admission) take you up the tower and onto
the balcony – in fine weather you can see as
far as the Blasket Islands and Connemara.
There's been a lighthouse here since 1670;
the present structure dates from 1854. It was
converted to electricity in 1871 and auto-
mated in 1991.

**★ Loop Head Summer
Hedge School** ARTS & CRAFTS
(☎ 086 819 7726; www.carmeltmadigan.com;
Cross Village; per 1/2/3/4 days €75/100/270/310;
⊗ early Jul–mid-Aug) Occasional seashore
safaris (adult/family €20/60) feature
among the acclaimed courses led by
local artist, writer and naturalist Carmel
Madigan. They'll see you immersed in the
landscape and developing new skills and
knowledge encompassing everything from
stone art and paintings to habitats, seaweed
and sealife.

Loop Head Walking Tours WALKING
(☎ 086 826 0987; www.loopheadwalkingtours.ie;
from €25; ⊗ by request) Friendly local expert
Martin runs guided walks around the peninsula's cliffs and lanes, ranging from a
couple of hours to a half-day hike to Loop
Head Lighthouse itself. Email ahead to see if
there's room on a tour.

Dolphinwatch CRUISE
(☎ 065-905 8156; www.dolphinwatch.ie; The
Square, Carrigaholt; tours adult/child €35/20;
⊗ Apr-Oct) Some 200 resident bottlenose

The round tower at Scattery Island (p97)
WESLEY COWPAR/SHUTTERSTOCK ©

dolphins frolic in the Shannon Estuary; they're best encountered on Dolphinwatch's two-hour cruises, on which you might also see minke and fin whales in autumn. Sailings depend on tides and weather conditions. Boats depart from Carrigaholt's Castle Pier; it's best to park by Dolphinwatch's booking office a few hundred metres away, as accessing the pier itself by car is tricky.

Dolphinwatch also runs Loop Head sunset cruises and geology tours.

🛏 Sleeping & Eating

Pure Camping   CAMPGROUND €
(☑ 065-905 7953; www.purecamping.ie; Querrin; pitches per 2 adults €24, bell tents €60-85, cabins €90-105; ⊙ May-Sep) It's luxury all the way at this boutique campsite tucked in among the Loop Head fields. To spacious pitches, furnished canvas bell tents and four-person wooded cabins, add yoga classes, a pizza oven and a sauna. And all just a 15-minute walk from the sea.

★ Loop Head Lighthouse
Keeper's Cottage   COTTAGE €€
(☑ 01-670 4733; www.irishlandmark.com; Loop Head; 2 nights €460-548) Staying at the former Loop Head Lighthouse keeper's home gives you a real feel for what life was once like out here. Managed by the Irish Landmark Trust, the 19th-century cottage sleeps five, and has no TV or wi-fi – all the better then for

enjoying the radio, books, board games and warming wood stove.

★ Long Dock   SEAFOOD €€
(☑ 065-905 8106; www.thelongdock.com; West St, Carrigaholt; mains €12-25; ⊙ 11am-9pm, closed Mon-Wed Nov-Feb) With stone walls and floors, and a roaring fire, this treasure of a pub has a seriously good kitchen. Seafood is the order of the day – you'll see the folks who work out in the estuary drinking at the bar. Specialities include Loop Head monkfish, Carrigaholt crab, Shannon Estuary sea bass and house-cured salmon, along with sensational chowder.

🛍 Shopping

Kilbaha Gallery & Crafts   ARTS & CRAFTS
(☑ 065-905 8843; www.kilbahagallery.com; R487, Kilbaha; ⊙ 10am-6pm daily Mar-Sep, Sat & Sun Oct-Dec; 🛜) Paintings, sculptures, photography, crafts, books and postcards at this delightful shop are all made by local artists. Up the back, its little light-filled cafe (dishes from €3) serves fantastic coffee, cakes, scones with homemade jam and freshly churned cream, herbal teas and warming hot chocolate.

Miltown Malbay
POP 829

Miltown Malbay has a thriving music scene and hosts the annual Willie Clancy Summer School, one of Ireland's great traditional music events.

An Ghiolla Finn Gift Shop (☑ 065-708 5107; Main St; ⊙ 10.30am-5pm Mon-Sat mid-Mar–Oct) doubles as the tourist office. It also opens on some summer Sundays.

Spanish Point   BEACH
See p20.

★ Coast Lodge   INN €€
(☑ 065-708 5687; www.coastlodge.ie; R482, Spanish Point; d/f/apt from €126/136/140; ℗🛜) Opposite the beach at Spanish Point, this beautifully appointed inn has luxurious rooms overlooking the ocean or adjacent golf course. Although the cottage-style apartments don't have standout views, they come with spacious lounges, full kitchens, laundries and patios with picnic tables.

Craft beers are served at the piano bar; the attached restaurant (mains €14 to €17) serves upmarket, seafood-focused bistro fare.

CLARE'S OTHER CLIFFS

On the way to and from the southern tip of Loop Head, take in the jaw-dropping sea vistas and drama of the sensational cliffs along the coast roads.

Heading west, from Carrigaholt drive south down central Church St for around 2km till you reach a junction with brown Loop Head Drive signs pointing right. This scenic route is the Coast Rd (L2002). It bounces beside a rocky shore, past reed beds and alongside green fields, offering splendid panoramas of the sea. It runs through the village of Rhinevilla, eventually rejoining the R487 at Kilbaha before surging onto the lighthouse at Loop Head.

Heading east from Loop Head Lighthouse, drive back along the R487 for a few minutes until signs point left along another Coast Rd (L2000). From here you make your way to Kilkee. You'll rejoin the R487 but can head north again along small roads north from just after either Oughterard or Cross for stunning views of soaring coastal cliffs.

Old Bake House   BISTRO €€
(☑ 065-708 4350; www.theoldbakehouse.ie; Main St; mains lunch €5-14, dinner €17-27; ⊙noon-9pm Sun-Thu, to 10pm Fri & Sat, reduced winter hours) Blackboard menus line the walls at the Old Bake House, which serves light dishes like soup and open sandwiches at lunch and dinner mains including salmon with creamed leek, and Moroccan spiced chicken. Live music plays on Fridays and Saturdays from 7pm.

Hillery's   PUB
See p20.

Friel's Bar   PUB
See p20.

❶ Getting There & Away

Bus Éireann (www.buseireann.ie) bus 333 runs once a day, Monday to Saturday, north and south along the coast, taking in Spanish Point beach (€3, five minutes), and heading inland to Ennis (€15, 1¼ hours).

Ennistimon

POP 1045

◉ Sights & Activities

★ **Cascades**   WATERFALL
See p20.

Courthouse Studios & Gallery   ARTS CENTRE
(☑ 065-707 1630; www.thecourthousegallery.com; Parliament St; ⊙noon-5pm Tue-Sat May-Sep, to 4pm Nov-May) FREE Rotating exhibitions from local and international artists are displayed over two floors of these studios, which are located in a renovated 19th-century courthouse.

🛏 Sleeping & Eating

The town features some superb eateries, with restaurants and cafes congregating along Main St. The **farmers market** (Market Sq; ⊙10am-2pm Sat) 🍴 sets up weekly on Market Sq.

★ **Byrne's Inn**   INN €€
(☑ 065-707 1080; www.byrnes-ennistymon.ie; Main St; d from €105; P 🛜) Facing Main St out front and the rushing waters of the town's Cascades out back, this historic guesthouse has one of Ennistimon's most colourful facades, in vibrant shades of violet, orange, aqua and sky-blue. Up the steep stairs are six large, stylish, contemporary rooms – some with Cascades views.

Downstairs, its **restaurant** (☑ 065-707 1080; www.byrnes-ennistymon.ie; Main St; mains lunch €5-16, dinner €8-24; ⊙10am-9pm, closed Mon Oct-Mar; 🛜) is the town's best.

Falls Hotel   HOTEL €€
(☑ 065-707 1004; www.fallshotel.ie; off N67; s/d/f/tr €100/150/190/225; P 🛜🏊) Built on the ruins of an O'Brien castle on the western edge of town, the vast, Georgian Falls Hotel was once the family home of Caitlín MacNamara, who married Dylan Thomas. Today it houses a large indoor pool, a spa and 142 modern rooms overlooking the rushing River Inagh and 20 hectares of wooded grounds.

★ **Cheese Press**   DELI €
(☑ 085 760 7037; Main St; ⊙8am-6pm Mon-Sat) Everything you need for a riverside picnic or a packed lunch for a Burren hike is on offer at this enticing deli. Organic Irish cheeses include **St Tola Irish goat cheese** (☑ 065-683 6633; www.st-tola.ie; off L1094, Inagh; adult/child €10/5; ⊙tours by reservation) 🍴, Abbey

Brie, Ballyhooly Blue, Burren Gold, Smoked Gubbeen and Bay Lough Cheddar. It also has smoked salmon and hams, relishes and house-baked bread, and the best coffee in town.

Oh La La   CRÊPES €
(☑ 065-707 2500; Parliament St; galettes €6-13, crêpes €3.50-8; ☺ 10am-5pm Mon-Sat, 11am-5pm Sun; ☑ 🐾) At this brightly coloured little crêperie, savoury buckwheat galettes include Clonakilty black pudding with apple compote and crème fraiche, and Burren smoked salmon with capers and leeks. Sweet crêpes span chestnut cream with honey-roasted cashews to white chocolate with rhubarb jam.

Drinking & Nightlife

Ennistimon's wonderful old pubs are a highlight of a visit. Trad sessions take place most nights in summer and regularly throughout the rest of the year.

★ Eugene's   PUB
See p21.

Cooley's House   PUB
See p21.

Shopping

★ Irish Hand Weaves   ARTS & CRAFTS
(☑ 087 648 5937; www.irishhandweaves.ie; Main St; ☺ 10am-5pm Tue-Fri, 11am-5pm Sat, to 4pm Sun) You'll likely find weaver Jean Moran behind her loom in this studio-workshop, surrounded by her creations. Browse local craftspeople's work, or learn the skills yourself in her spinning and weaving taster sessions (from €30).

Cliffs of Moher

In good visibility, the Cliffs of Moher (Aillte an Mothair, or Ailltreacha Mothair) are staggeringly beautiful. The entirely vertical cliffs rise to a height of 214m, their edge abruptly falling away into a ceaselessly churning Atlantic.

 THE ATM HUNT

It's easy to get caught cashless in western Clare. Many small towns are ATM-free zones, so stock up with money when you can. You'll find ATMs in Ennistimon, Kilkee, Kilrush and Lahinch.

In a progression of vast heads, the dark sandstone and siltstone strata march in a rigid formation. Views stretch to the Aran Islands and the hills of Connemara. Sunsets here see the sky turn a kaleidoscope of amber, amethyst, rose pink and deep garnet red.

One of Ireland's blockbuster sights, it includes a high-tech visitor centre, a 19th-century lookout tower and a wealth of walking trails. Visiting by boat can bring the best views.

The cliffs' fame guarantees a steady stream of visitors, which can surge in summer – up to 10,000 people on busy August bank-holiday weekends. But the tireless Atlantic winds, and expansive walking options, help thin out the crowds. A vast, grass-covered visitor centre with innovative exhibits, is embedded into the side of a hill. The main walkways and viewing areas along the cliffs have a 1.5m-high wall to prevent visitors getting too close to the crumbling, often slippery edge.

You're rewarded with epic views if you walk even a short way north or south along the cliffs. Note the hiking trails are strenuous, encompassing narrow, exposed cliff paths with steep ascents and descents. Proper boots and kit are a must.

To the north, you can follow the **Doolin Trail**, via the 1835-built stone observation post **O'Brien's Tower** (☑ 065-708 6141; www. cliffsofmoher.ie; Cliffs of Moher; adult/child €2/1; ☺ hours vary), to the village of Doolin (8km; 2½ hours).

Heading south, past the end of the 'Moher Wall', a 5km trail runs along the cliffs to **Hag's Head** – few venture this far, yet the views are uninhibited. Forming the southern end of the Cliffs of Moher, Hag's Head is a dramatic place from which to view the cliffs. There's a huge sea arch at the tip of Hag's Head and another arch visible to the north. The old signal tower on the head was erected in case Napoleon tried to attack the western coast of Ireland. From Hag's Head, you can continue on to Liscannor for a total walk of just under 12km (about 3½ hours).

The entire 20km-long Liscannor to Doolin walking path via the cliffs is signposted as the **Cliffs of Moher Coastal Walk**; it's likely to take four to five hours. Seasonal **shuttle buses** (☑ 065-707 5599; www.cliffsof-mohercoastalwalk.ie; one-way €8; ☺ 6 services daily, Mar-Oct; 🐾) link stops along this route.

Look out for migrating minke and humpback whales in autumn. With binoculars you can spot the more than 30 species of birds – including adorable puffins, which appear between mid-March and mid-July.

For awe-inspiring views of the cliffs and wildlife, consider a **cruise**. Boat operators in Doolin, including Doolin 2 Aran Ferries (p102) and the Doolin Ferry Co (p102), offer popular tours of the cliffs.

The cliffs are enabled with free wi-fi. It's possible to exit (but not enter) the car park once it closes for the day.

Cliffs of Moher Visitor Centre VISITOR CENTRE (☑ 065-708 6141; www.cliffsofmoher.ie; R478; adult/child incl parking €8/free; ⊙ 8am-9pm May-Aug, to 7pm Mar, Apr, Sep & Oct, 9am-5pm Nov-Feb) Covered in turf and cut into the hillside, the cliffs' state-of-the-art visitor centre has engaging exhibitions covering the fauna, flora, geology and climate of the cliffs, and an interactive genealogy board with information on local family names. Free information booklets on the cliffs are available, or download the app (also free) online. Booking an off-peak visit (8am to 11am and 4pm to close) online, 24 hours in advance, brings the adult entrance fee down to €4.

THE BURREN

Stretching across northern Clare, the rocky, windswept Burren region is a unique striated lunar-like landscape of barren grey limestone that was shaped beneath ancient seas, then forced high and dry by a great geological cataclysm. It covers 250 sq km of exposed limestone, and 560 sq km in total.

Wildflowers in spring give the Burren brilliant, if ephemeral, colour amid its stark beauty. Villages throughout the region include the music hub of Doolin on the west coast, Kilfenora inland and charming Ballyvaughan in the north, on the shores of Galway Bay.

South of Ballyvaughan, a series of severe bends twists up **Corkscrew Hill** (180m), which was built as part of a Great Famine relief scheme in the 1840s. Nearby photogenic prehistoric sites include **Gleninsheen Wedge Tomb** (R480) FREE, **Poulnabrone Dolmen** (R480) FREE and **Caherconnell Fort** (☑ 065-708 9999; www.caherconnell.com; R480; adult/child €6/4, sheepdog demonstration €5/3, combination ticket €9.60/5.60; ⊙ 10am-6pm Jul & Aug, to 5.30pm May, Jun & Sep, 10.30am-5pm mid-Mar–Apr & Oct).

❶ DODGING THE CROWDS AT THE CLIFFS OF MOHER

As with many dramatic natural sights, lots of people (naturally) want to visit. Luckily it really is possible to dodge the coach-party crowds.

Board a Boat Yes, you're still surrounded by people, but seeing the 214m cliffs from the bottom makes the crowds feel small. Book trips from nearby Doolin.

Hike from Doolin It takes 2½ hours minimum to walk from Doolin along difficult, exposed trails. But if you're fit and have the right kit, you'll love it.

Moher Walk Another challenging hike for the well-equipped; a 5km trail from the visitor centre south to spectacular Hag's Head.

Walk 20 Minutes Many visitors gather at the main viewing platform; walking south takes you to a puffin-viewing spot and, beyond, fewer crowds.

Throughout the region, there are fantastic opportunities for walking and rock climbing.

🏃 Activities

The Burren is a walker's paradise. The stark, beautiful landscape, plentiful trails and ancient sites are best explored on foot. 'Green roads' are the old highways of the Burren, crossing hills and valleys to some of the remotest corners of the region. Many of these unpaved ways were built during the Famine as part of relief work, while some may date back thousands of years. Now used mostly by hikers and the occasional farmer, some are signposted.

Beginning in Lahinch and ending in Corofin, the **Burren Way** is a 123km waymarked network of walking routes along a mix of roads, lanes and paths. There are also seven waymarked trails through the national park, taking from 30 minutes to three hours to hike.

Guided nature, history, archaeology and wilderness walks are great ways to appreciate this unique region. Typically the cost of the walks averages €10 to €35 and there are many options, including private trips. Operators include Burren Guided Walks & Hikes (p102), Heart of Burren Walks (p102) and Burren Wild Tours (p102).

The **Burren National Park** (www.burrennationalpark.ie) also runs free guided walks;

WORTH A TRIP

ST TOLA GOAT CHEESE

Creamy St Tola Irish goat's cheese (p99) is served at some of Ireland's finest restaurants, with award-winning lines including ash log, Greek-style feta and Gouda-style hard cheese. Call ahead to the farm to see if you can join a tour on which you'll pet the goats, watch them being fed, see a cheese-making demonstration and taste the products. The farm is 11km southeast of Ennistimon (16km northwest of Ennis), signposted off the N85.

its website lists dates and has a downloadable hiking map.

Burren Wild Tours　　　　　WALKING
($\boxed{2}$087 877 9565; www.burrenwalks.com; €35; ⊙by appointment) John Connolly offers a broad range of walks, from gentle to more strenuous. Themes include heritage, botany and folklore.

Heart of Burren Walks　　　　WALKING
($\boxed{2}$087 292 5487; www.heartofburrenwalks.com; €30; ⊙by reservation Tue-Sat) Local Burren author Tony Kirby leads walks and archaeology hikes lasting 2½ hours. Cash only.

Burren Guided Walks & Hikes　　WALKING
($\boxed{2}$065-707 6100, 087 244 6807; www.burrenguidedwalks.com; from €20; ⊙by reservation) Longtime guide Mary Howard leads groups on a variety of rambles, off-the-beaten-track hikes and rugged routes.

ⓘ Information

BOOKS & MAPS

There is a wealth of literature about the Burren. In Ennis' bookshops and local visitor centres, look out for publications such as Charles Nelson's *Wild Plants of the Burren and the Aran Islands*. The *Burren Journey* books by George Cunningham are excellent for local lore. *The Burren and the Aran Islands: A Walking Guide* by Tony Kirby is an excellent, up-to-date resource.

The Burren Series of Ramblers' Guides and Maps published by Tír Eolas (www.tireolas.com) features three illustrated, fold-out maps: *Ballyvaughan* (€4), *Kilfenora* (€3) and *O'Brien Country* (€3; which covers Doolin, Lisdoonvarna and the Cliffs of Moher). The booklet *The Burren Way* has good walking routes. Ordnance Survey Ireland Discovery series maps 51 and 57 cover most of the area.

VISITOR INFORMATION

The Burren Centre (p106) in Kilfenora is an excellent resource, as are the Burren **Tourist Office** ($\boxed{2}$065-682 7693; www.burrennational park.ie; Clare Heritage Centre, Church St; ⊙9.30am-5pm Apr-Sep) and the Clare Heritage & Genealogy Centre in Corofin.

Online, informative sites include the following:
Burren Ecotourism (www.burren.ie)
Burren Geopark (www.burrengeopark.ie)
Burren National Park (www.burrennational park.ie)
Burrenbeo Trust (www.burrenbeo.com)

Doolin

POP 280

Located 6km northeast of the Cliffs of Moher in a landscape riddled with caves and laced with walking paths, Doolin is a jumping-off point for cliff cruises and ferries out to the Aran Islands.

Without a centre, this scattered settlement consists of three smaller linked villages. Charming **Fisherstreet** has some picturesque traditional cottages; there are dramatic surf vistas at the harbour 1.5km west along the coast. **Doolin** itself is about 1km east on the little River Aille. **Roadford** is another 1km east. None of the villages has more than a handful of buildings.

While the music pubs give Doolin a lively vibe, the heavy concentration of visitors means standards don't always hold up to those in some of Clare's less-frequented villages (p107).

◉ Sights & Activities

Doolin Pier is the departure point for memorable, one-hour cruises to the 214m Cliffs of Moher, 6km to the southwest. They're recommended not only for views of towering cliffs that loom ever-closer, but also great wildlife-spotting opportunities. **Doolin 2 Aran Ferries** ($\boxed{2}$065-707 5949; www.doolin2aranferries.com; Doolin Pier; €15; ⊙mid-Mar–Oct) and the **Doolin Ferry Co** ($\boxed{2}$065-707 5555; www.doolinferry.com; Doolin Pier; €15; ⊙mid-Mar–Oct) are two firms running popular trips.

★Doolin Cave　　　　　　CAVE
($\boxed{2}$065-707 5761; www.doolincave.ie; R479; adult/child €15/8; ⊙10am-6pm Mar-Oct, 11am-4pm Sat & Sun Nov-early Jan) The Great Stalactite, the longest in Europe at 7.3m, is the big draw of Doolin Cave. Tour times vary seasonally, but

are usually on the hour. Glacial clay from deep within the cave is used by on-site potter Caireann Browne, who sells her works here. The property also has a 1km-long farmland trail featuring rare animal breeds, and a cafe.

The caves are around 4km north of town. Tickets are 20% cheaper if bought online in advance.

Doonagore Castle CASTLE
(off R478) Looking every inch a fairy-tale stronghold, round, turreted Doonagore Castle dates from the 16th century. The ruin was restored by architect Percy Leclerc in the 1970s for an American client whose family still owns it. The interior is closed to the public, but aim to pass by at sunset for photos set against a multihued sky. It's some 2km south of Doolin.

Doolin Cliff Walk WALKING
(🖉065-707 4170; www.doolincliffwalk.com; €10; ⊙10am May–early Nov) This tremendous three-hour cliff walk sets off each morning from outside Gus O'Connor's pub in Fisherstreet past Doonagore Castle, ending at the Cliffs of Moher Visitor Centre (p101), from where you can get a bus back to Doolin. Due to the precipitous terrain, it's not recommended for kids or anyone with limited mobility or vertigo.

🎇 Festivals & Events

Russell Memorial Weekend MUSIC
(🖉065-707 4168; www.michorussellweekend.ie; ⊙Feb) Held on the last weekend in February, this festival celebrates the work of legendary Doolin musician Micho Russell and his brothers, and features workshops, dancing classes and trad-music sessions throughout town.

🛌 Sleeping

Doolin has scores of good-value hostels and B&Bs. If you're planning on catching trad-music sessions, choose your location carefully, as you may find yourself staying a very long way from the pubs you most want to visit, and roads in the area are narrow and unlit.

★**Doolin Inn & Hostel** HOSTEL €
(🖉087 282 0587; www.doolinhostel.ie; Fisherstreet; dm/d/tr/q from €30/75/90/125; 🅿@🛜) In a great Fisherstreet location, this friendly, family-run property is split between two neighbouring buildings. On

Doolin
GIMAS/SHUTTERSTOCK ©

the hill, the main building houses the inn, with immaculate, neutrally toned B&B accommodation, reception and a great cafe stocking craft beers. The hostel, with five- to 12-bed dorms, is directly across the street.

No hen or stag parties ensure a low-key, sociable atmosphere.

Aille River Hostel HOSTEL €
(🖉065-707 4260; www.ailleriverhosteldoolin.ie; Doolin; dm €21-23, d €52-58, campsites per adult €10; ⊙Mar-Dec; 🅿🛜) In a picturesque spot by the river, this converted, cosy, 17th-century farmhouse is a great choice, with peat fires and free laundry. There are 24 beds and a camping area; if you don't have your own tent, ask about tepee rental.

Rainbow Hostel HOSTEL €
(🖉065-707 4415; rainbowhostel@eircom.net; Roadford; dm/d/tr from €20/50/66; 🅿🛜) With a lovely stove in its lounge, wooden ceilings and colourful rooms, this cottagey IHH-affiliated hostel has 24 beds in an old farmhouse by the road. It also rents out bikes (€10 per day).

Nagles Camping & Caravan Park CAMPGROUND €
(🖉065-707 4458; www.doolincamping.com; Fisherstreet; campsites per 2 adults €20; ⊙mid-Mar–mid-Oct; 🅿🛜) Let the nearby pounding surf lull you to sleep at this grassy expanse 100m from the pier. The spaces for

caravans, campervans and tents are open to the elements, so pin those pegs down hard. Timber glamping pods (from €70) have a small double bed, single bed, kitchenette and porch.

★ O'Connors Guesthouse
& Riverside Camping   INN €€

(☑ 065-707 4498; www.oconnorsdoolin.com; Doolin; s €55-70, d €70-100, campsites per 2 adults €16-20; ⊗ late Feb-Nov; 🅿🛜) On a bend in the River Aille, this working farm has an L-shaped barn-style guesthouse with 10 spick-and-span rooms, two of which are equipped for visitors with limited mobility. Next door, tent pitches, and caravan and campervan sites, some right by the river, are available at its campground, along with glamping yurts, tepees and cool retro caravans (€80 to €100).

Twin Peaks   B&B €€

(☑ 086-812 7049; www.twinpeaksdoolin.com; Fisherstreet; s/d €65/90; 🅿🛜) The rural views and soothing feel at this simple but smart B&B belie the fact that it's just a few minutes' walk from Fisherstreet's huddle of shops and pubs. Warmly welcoming hosts who're happy to advise on the best places to eat and drink are another plus.

Cullinan's Guesthouse   INN €€

(☑ 065-707 4183; www.cullinansdoolin.com; Doolin; d €120-140; ⊗ Mar-Nov; 🅿🛜) Owned by well-known fiddle-playing James Cullinan, this mustard-coloured inn on the River Aille has eight spotless, comfortable, pine-furnished rooms. A couple of rooms are slightly smaller than the others, but have river views.

It has a lovely back terrace for enjoying the views and a well-regarded restaurant.

Sea View House   B&B €€

(☑ 087 267 9617; www.seaview-doolin.ie; Fisherstreet; d €120-200; ⊗ mid-Mar–Oct; 🅿🛜) Sweeping views extend from higher-priced rooms at this aptly named house on high ground above Fisherstreet village, and from the timber deck. Rooms have dark wood furniture, floral curtains and colourful prints; the common lounge has a telescope for surveying the panorama.

Hotel Doolin   HOTEL €€

(☑ 065-707 4111; www.hoteldoolin.ie; Doolin; d/f/tr €145/188/205; 🅿🛜) 🌿 The supremely comfortable, streamlined rooms at this contemporary hotel have elegant dark-wood furniture and Voya Irish seaweed toiletries. On the ground floor, the stylish lounge opens to a patio and lawns. Look out for deals online.

✖ Eating

Irish classics such as bacon and cabbage and seafood chowder are served at Doolin's pubs throughout the day until about 9.30pm. Doolin also has a handful of restaurants and cafes, some open only in summer.

There are no supermarkets (or ATMs), so stock up on supplies before you arrive.

Doolin Cafe   CAFE €

(☑ 065-707 4795; www.doolincafe.ie; Roadford; mains €3.50-11; ⊗ 9am-6pm Wed-Mon mid-Mar-late Oct; ✏🦽) Locals love to gather at the picnic tables outside the Doolin Cafe – a white-painted cottage with purple trim. Bumper breakfasts are served until 1pm and include vegan, vegetarian and seafood options. Soups and salads star at lunch, while pastries and cakes tempt you throughout the day.

Cullinan's   MODERN IRISH €€€

(☑ 065-707 4183; www.cullinansdoolin.com; Doolin; mains €22-29; ⊗ 6-9pm Mon, Tue & Thu-Sat Easter–mid-Oct) The brief menu at this superb restaurant is accompanied by a long wine list. Dishes change depending on what's fresh, but expect plates such as baked monkfish with almond pesto, marinated Burren lamb, and brandy-poached strawberry and mascarpone crème brûlée. Book.

🍷 Drinking & Entertainment

Doolin's famed music pubs – Gus O'Connor's in Fisherstreet and McGann's and McDermott's in Roadford – have sessions throughout the year, as does Fitz's. To experience trad music in the intimate surrounds of an Irish home, reserve ahead to visit the Doolin Music House.

★ Gus O'Connor's   PUB
See p24.

McGann's   PUB
See p24.

McDermott's   PUB
See p24.

Fitz's
PUB

(☑065-707 4111; www.hoteldoolin.ie; Doolin; ☺noon-11.30pm Mon-Thu, to 12.30am Fri & Sat, to 11pm Sun) At Hotel Doolin, relative newcomer Fitz's has trad sessions twice nightly from April to October and at least three times a week from November to March. Sample its superb whiskey selection, fine craft beers and ciders, or own-brewed Dooliner beer.

Bar food (mains €9 to €24) is first rate. Ingenious cocktails include MV Plassy on the Rocks, named after the **Aran Islands shipwreck**, a Burren martini and a Father Jack Espresso (in honour of the cantankerous priest from *Father Ted*).

★ Doolin Music House
TRADITIONAL MUSIC

(☑086 824 1085; www.doolinmusichouse. com; R478, Caherkinalla; €20; ☺by reservation 7-8.30pm Mon, Wed & Fri) For a change from Doolin's crowded music pubs, book ahead to visit local musician Christy Barry's cosy home, which is filled with artworks by his artist partner Sheila. By the open fire, Christy plays traditional tunes, tells stories relating to Irish musical history and welcomes questions. The price includes a glass of wine and snacks. It's 4km east of Doolin.

🛍 Shopping

Clare Jam Shop
FOOD

(☑065-707 4778; www.clare-jam-shop.business. site; off R478; ☺9am-6pm) 🍴 Jams (such as wild blueberry; strawberry and champagne; and blackberry and apple), marmalades (including Irish whiskey), jellies (such as rose petal), chutneys (tomato and rhubarb) and mustards (including Guinness mustard) are homemade using traditional open-pan boiling methods at this sweet little hilltop cottage 3.5km southwest of Fisherstreet (3km north of the Cliffs of Moher). Many ingredients are handpicked in the Burren.

Doolin Chocolate Shop
CHOCOLATE

(☑061-922 080; www.wildeirishchocolates.com; Fisherstreet; ☺11am-7pm May-Oct, shorter hours Nov-Apr) Lavender and rose, seaweed and lime, and hazelnut and raisin are among the chocolate flavours made by Clare company Wilde Irish Chocolates, which has its **factory** (☑061-922 080; www.wildeirishchocolates. com; Tuamgraney; ☺by arrangement) FREE in Tuamgraney near Lough Derg in the county's east. This shop also sells white and dark chocolate spreads, and fudge such as porter or Irish cream liqueur.

❶ Information

The town's **tourist information point** (☑065-707 5649; Doolin; ☺8am-8pm Easter-Sep) is alongside the central Hotel Doolin. The website www.doolin.ie has comprehensive tourist information.

❶ Getting There & Away

From mid-March to October, **Doolin Pier** (off R439) is one of two ferry departure points to the Aran Islands (the other is **Rossaveal Ferry Terminal** (Rossaveal), 37km west of Galway city, where services are year-round). Sailings can be affected if high seas or tides make the small dock inaccessible.

Doolin 2 Aran Ferries (p102) and **Doolin Ferry Co** (p102) each have sailings to Inisheer (one way/return €10/20, 30 minutes, three to four daily), Inishmore (€15/25, 1¼ hours, two to three daily) and Inishmaan (€15/25, from 45 minutes, two to three daily). Interisland ferry tickets cost €10 to €15 per crossing.

There are various combination tickets and online discounts.

Lisdoonvarna

POP 829

For centuries people have been visiting Lisdoonvarna (Lios Dún Bhearna) for its mineral springs. The village is more down at heel today than in its Victorian heyday, but it makes a good base for exploring the area.

◉ Sights & Activities

Burren Smokehouse
FOOD

See p24.

DON'T MISS

LISDOONVARNA MATCHMAKING FESTIVAL

Lisdoonvarna was once a centre for *basadóiri* (matchmakers) who, for a fee, would fix up a person with a spouse. Most of the (mainly male) hopefuls would hit town in September, feet shuffling, cap in hand, after the hay was in. Today, the **Lisdoonvarna Matchmaking Festival** (☑065-707 4005; www. matchmakerireland.com; ☺weekends Sep) is billed as Europe's largest singles' festival, with music, dancing and partying on September weekends.

COUNTY CLARE LISDOONVARNA

Leamaneh Castle, Kilfenora
T.SLACK/SHUTTERSTOCK ©

Spa Well SPRING

At the town's southern end is a spa well, with a sulphur spring, a Victorian pump-house and a wooded setting. The iron, sulphur, magnesium and iodine in the water are believed to be good for rheumatic and glandular complaints.

Walking trails head off east beside the river to two other well sites. They emerge, handily, near the Roadside Tavern (p23) and the Burren Smokehouse (p24).

🛏 Sleeping & Eating

Lisdoonvarna has a hostel and a couple of inns. Book ahead if you're heading here for the **Father Ted Festival** (www.tedtours.com; ⊙ early May), on the May bank holiday weekend, or September's Matchmaking Festival (p105).

Sleepzone Burren Hostel HOSTEL €

(☑ 065-707 4036; www.sleepzone.ie; Kincora Rd; dm/d/f €19/70/90; P 🛜) The rooms in this modern, friendly hostel set in a former hotel range from six-bed dorms to family rooms that sleep up to five people. Facilities include a self-catering kitchen, a book-filled guest lounge and a large lawn.

★ Sheedy's Hotel & Restaurant INN €€

(☑ 065-707 4026; www.sheedys.com; Main St; d from €150; ⊙ mid-Mar–Sep; P 🛜) Stately 18th-century country house Sheedy's has 11 beautifully furnished rooms with checked fabrics and sage-coloured walls. The long

front porch has comfy chairs for looking out over the gardens. Nonguests are welcome at its restaurant (mains €18 to €29), which serves dinner Monday to Saturday, 6.30pm to 8.30pm by reservation, and its bar, which has a huge range of whiskeys.

Whiskey-soaked porridge with Baileys is on the menu at breakfast.

Wild Honey Inn INN €€

(☑ 065-707 4300; www.wildhoneyinn.com; Kincora Rd; d €140-185; ⊙ early Mar-Nov; P 🛜) In an 1840s roadside mansion, Wild Honey has 14 stylish rooms, some opening onto private terraces overlooking the gardens. Its acclaimed restaurant (three courses from €44) serves seasonal dishes teaming French flair with Irish ingredients (dinner from 6pm Wednesday to Saturday, plus Tuesday May to September).

★ Roadside Tavern PUB

See p23.

Kilfenora

POP 175

Kilfenora (Cill Fhionnúrach) lies on the southern fringe of the Burren, 8.5km southeast of Lisdoonvarna. It's a small place, with low polychromatic buildings surrounding the compact centre.

◉ Sights

Burren Centre MUSEUM

(☑ 065-708 8030; www.theburrencentre.ie; Main St; adult/child €6/4; ⊙ 9.30am-5.30pm Jun-Aug, 10am-5pm Mar-May, Sep & Oct) At the Burren Centre, a 12-minute film gives you an overview of the Burren's flora, fauna and geology, while interactive exhibits detail its formation and evolution right up to the present day. Exhibits also cover the Kilfenora Céilí Band. You'll also find a tearoom and a large shop stocking Irish-made crafts.

Kilfenora Cathedral RUINS

See p21.

Leamaneh Castle RUINS

(junction R476 & R480) This magnificent, allegedly haunted ruin stands on a rise 6.2km east of Kilfenora. Built in 1480 as a tower house and converted to a mansion in 1650, it's the erstwhile home of Máire Rúa (Red Mary) who – according to local anecdote – got through 25 husbands, dispatching at least one to a grisly death on horseback off the Cliffs of Moher, before being incarcerated in a hollow tree by her enemies.

Drinking & Nightlife

★ **Vaughan's Pub**   PUB
See p23.

Linnane's Pub   PUB
See p23.

Ballyvaughan & Around

POP 191

To the village's south, at the foothills of the Burren, you can visit the two-million-year-old **Aillwee Cave** (☑065-707 7036; www.aillweecave.ie; off R480; cave adult/child €11/5, raptor exhibit €9/7, combined ticket €17/10; ☺10am-6.30pm Jul & Aug, to 5.30pm Mar-Jun, Sep & Oct, to 5pm Nov-Feb), carved out by water some two million years ago. The main cave penetrates 600m into the mountain, widening into larger caverns, one with its own waterfall. Near the entrance are the remains of a brown bear, extinct in Ireland for over 10,000 years. Aillwee Cave has a cafe and a shop selling local Burren Gold cheese.

Sleeping & Eating

Ballyvaughan is one of the loveliest places to stay in the Burren. Several B&Bs and inns are close to the village centre.

Pubs in Ballyvaughan serve quality fare. It also has a daytime cafe and a small supermarket. Local produce is sold at the **farmers market** (☑087 647 2120; St John's Hall car park; ☺10am-2pm Sat May-Oct) 🍴.

★ **Wild Atlantic Lodge**   INN €€
(☑065-707 7003; www.thewildatlanticlodge.com; Main St; d/tr/f from €100/140/180; ❐🐕) The Wild Atlantic Lodge overflows with comfort and charm, from the soft woollen blankets in the warm-hued rooms to the huge Burren photographs covering the walls. Breakfast is served in its airy Wildflower Restaurant and Bar, which delivers a mellow soundtrack and outstanding food (mains €13 to €24); beef and lamb from its own farm are scented with Burren-foraged herbs.

You'll find it in the centre of Ballyvaughan village.

Cappabhaile House   B&B €€
(☑083 858 0018; www.cappabhaile.com; N67; d €110, f €130-155) At Cappabhaile House you sink into serenity. Set in 5 hectares of gorgeous Burren countryside 3km south of Ballyvaughan, it's surrounded by the sounds of birdsong and cows. Styling is country-life chic: quality furnishings in warm colours sit beside stripped floorboards and polished wood.

Breakfast treats include omelettes cooked to order and platters of Irish cheese.

Ballyvaughan Lodge   B&B €€
(☑065-707 7292; www.ballyvaughanlodge.com; N67; s/d €70/110; ❐🐕) Little touches make a big difference at Ballyvaughan Lodge: fragrant lilies, freshly ground coffee and breakfasts that include poached eggs and locally smoked salmon, and mushrooms on toast with blue cheese. Add polished floorboards, bright rugs and very comfy beds and you have a winner.

★ **Gregan's Castle Hotel**   HOTEL €€€
(☑065-707 7005; www.gregans.ie; N67; d €240-325, ste €377-447; ❐🐕) This hidden Clare gem is housed in a grand 18th-century manor, 5km south of Ballyvaughan at the aptly named, twisting Corkscrew Hill. The 21 rooms and suites combine antiques with contemporary countrified furnishings (and purposely no TVs); some open to private garden areas.

Nonguests are welcome by reservation at its glass-paned gourmet restaurant (four courses €75), which serves exquisite dishes like hand-dived barbecue scallops and wild garlic-laced Kilshanny lamb.

★ **Monks at the Pier**   SEAFOOD €€
(☑065-707 7059; www.monksballyvaughan.com; The Pier; mains €15-50; ☺noon-10pm Jun-Aug, to 9pm Sep-May) Although vegetarians and carnivores eat well here, seafood is the star at this whitewashed restaurant warmed by log-burning stoves. Think black Head Bay clams steamed in white wine; Burren smoked salmon and Liscannor crab salad; red ale-battered fish with triple-fried chips; natural and grilled oysters (per half dozen €12 to €16); and spectacular lobster (€50) and seafood platters (€32).

ⓘ Information

Inside a large gift shop behind the supermarket, Ballyvaughan's **visitor centre** (☑065-707 7464; www.ballyvaughantourism.com; N67; ☺10am-1.30pm & 2-6pm, reduced hours Oct-Apr) has a good selection of local guides and maps.

ROAD TRIP ESSENTIALS

Ireland Driving Guide

The motorway system makes for easy travelling between major towns, but the spidery network of secondary and tertiary roads makes for the most scenic driving.

DRIVING LICENCE & DOCUMENTS

EU licences are treated like Irish ones. Holders of non-EU licences from countries other than the US or Canada should obtain an International Driving Permit (IDP) from their home automobile association.

You must carry your driving licence at all times.

INSURANCE

All cars on public roads must be insured. Most hire companies quote basic insurance in their initial quote. If you are bringing your own vehicle, check that your insurance will cover you in Ireland. When driving your own car, you'll need a minimum insurance known as third-party insurance.

HIRING A CAR

Compared with many countries hire rates are expensive in Ireland; you should expect to pay around €250 a week for a small car (unlimited mileage), but rates go up at busy times and drop off in quieter seasons. The main players:

Avis (www.avis.ie)

Budget (www.budget.ie)

Europcar (www.europcar.ie)

Hertz (www.hertz.ie)

Sixt (www.sixt.ie)

Thrifty (www.thrifty.ie)

The major car-hire companies have different web pages on their websites for different countries, so the price of a car in Ireland can differ from the same car's price in the USA or Australia. You have to surf a lot of sites to get the best deals. **Nova Car Hire** (www.novacarhire. com) acts as an agent for Alamo, Budget, European and National, and offers greatly discounted rates.

➡ Most cars are manual; automatic cars are available, but they're more expensive to hire.

➡ If you're travelling from the Republic into Northern Ireland, it's important to be sure that your insurance covers journeys to the North.

➡ The majority of hire companies won't rent you a car if you're under 23 and haven't had a valid driving licence for at least a year.

➡ Some companies in the Republic won't rent to you if you're aged 74 or over; there's no upper age limit in the North.

➡ Motorbikes and mopeds are not available for hire in Ireland.

Driving Fast Facts

➡ **Right or left?** Drive on the left

➡ **Manual or automatic?** Manual

➡ **Legal driving age** 18

➡ **Top speed limit** 120km/h (motorways; 70mph in Northern Ireland)

➡ **Best radio station** RTE Radio 1

Ireland Playlist

Virtually every parish and hamlet has a song about it. Here are our favourites:

Carrickfergus Traditional Irish folk song

Galway Girl Steve Earle

Raglan Road Luke Kelly

Running to Stand Still U2

The Fields of Athenry Paddy Reilly

The Town I Loved So Well The Dubliners (about Derry)

BRINGING YOUR OWN VEHICLE

It's easy to take your own vehicle to Ireland and there are no specific procedures involved, but you should carry a vehicle registration document as proof that it's yours.

MAPS

You'll need a good road map; we recommend getting one even if you have a sat-nav system.

Michelin's 1:400,000-scale Ireland map (No 923) is a decent single-sheet map, with clear cartography and most of the island's scenic roads marked. The four maps (North, South, East and West) that make up the Ordnance Survey Holiday map series at 1:250,000 scale are useful if you want more detail. Collins also publishes a range of maps covering Ireland.

The Ordnance Survey Discovery series covers the whole island in 89 maps at a scale of 1:50,000.

These are all available at most big bookshops and tourist centres throughout Ireland as well as at www.osi.ie.

ROADS CONDITIONS

Irish road types and conditions vary wildly. The road network is divided into the following categories:

Regional Roads Indicated by an R and (usually) three numbers on a white background, these are the secondary and tertiary roads that make up the bulk of the road network, generally splintering off larger roads to access even the smallest hamlet. Blind corners, potholes and a width barely enough for two cars are the price for some of the most scenic routes in all of Ireland; whatever you do, go slow. In Northern Ireland, these are classified as B-roads.

Road Distances (Km)

	Athlone	Belfast	Cork	Derry	Donegal	Dublin	Galway	Kilkenny	Killarney	Limerick	Rosslare Harbour	Shannon Airport	Sligo	Waterford
Belfast	227													
Cork	219	424												
Derry	209	117	428											
Donegal	183	180	402	69										
Dublin	127	167	256	237	233									
Galway	93	306	209	272	204	212								
Kilkenny	116	284	148	335	309	114	172							
Killarney	232	436	87	441	407	304	193	198						
Limerick	121	323	105	328	296	193	104	113	111					
Rosslare Harbour	201	330	208	397	391	153	274	98	275	211				
Shannon Airport	133	346	128	351	282	218	93	135	135	25	234			
Sligo	117	206	336	135	66	214	138	245	343	232	325	218		
Waterford	164	333	126	383	357	163	220	48	193	129	82	152	293	
Wexford	184	309	187	378	372	135	253	80	254	190	19	213	307	61

National Roads Indicated by an N and two numbers against a green background, these were, until the construction of the motorway network, the primary roads in Ireland. They link most towns and are usually single lane in either direction, widening occasionally to double lane (usually on uphill stretches to allow for the overtaking of slower vehicles). In Northern Ireland, these are classified as A-roads.

Motorways Indicated by an M and a single digit against a blue background, the network is limited to the major routes and towns. Most motorways are partially tolled. Motorways in Northern Ireland are not tolled.

ROAD RULES

A copy of Ireland's road rules is available from tourist offices. Following are the most basic rules:

➡ Drive on the left, overtake to the right.

➡ Safety belts must be worn by the driver and all passengers.

➡ Children aged under 12 aren't allowed to sit on the front seats.

➡ Motorcyclists and their passengers must wear helmets.

➡ When entering a roundabout, give way to the right.

➡ On motorways, use the right lane for overtaking only.

➡ Speed limits are 120km/h on motorways (70mph in Northern Ireland), 100km/h on national roads (60mph in Northern Ireland), 80km/h on regional and local roads (60mph in Northern Ireland) and 50km/h (30mph in the North) or as signposted in towns.

➡ The legal alcohol limit is 50mg of alcohol per 100ml of blood or 22mg on the breath (roughly two units of alcohol for a man and one for a woman); in Northern Ireland the limit is 80mg of alcohol per 100ml of blood.

PARKING

All big towns and cities have covered and open short-stay car parks that are conveniently signposted.

➡ On-street parking is usually by 'pay and display' tickets available from on-street machines or disc parking (discs, which rotate to display the time you park your car, are usually provided

by rental agencies). Costs range from €1.50 to €6 per hour; all-day parking in a car park will cost around €25.

➡ Yellow lines (single or double) along the edge of the road indicate restrictions. Double yellow lines mean no parking at any time. Always look for the nearby sign that spells out when you can and cannot park.

➡ In Dublin, Cork and Galway, clamping is rigorously enforced; it'll cost you €85 to have the yellow beast removed. In Northern Ireland, the fee is £100 for removal.

FUEL

The majority of vehicles operate on unleaded petrol; the rest (including many hire cars) run on diesel.

Road Trip Websites

AUTOMOBILE ASSOCIATIONS

Automobile Association (AA; www.theaa.ie) Roadside assistance and driving tips.

Royal Automobile Club (RAC; www.rac.co.uk) Roadside assistance, route planner and accommodation.

ROAD RULES

Road Safety Authority (www.rsa.ie) Rules, tips and information in case of accident.

CONDITIONS & TRAFFIC

AA Roadwatch (www.theaa.ie) Up-to-date traffic info.

Traffic Watch Northern Ireland (www.trafficwatchni.com) Traffic news, maps and live cameras.

MAPS

AA Route Planner (www.theaa.ie) Map your route for the whole island.

APPS

Both the AA and the RAC have mobile apps for Android and IOS that track traffic and allow you to report breakdowns.

Cost In the Republic, petrol costs range from €1.30 to €1.50 per litre, with diesel usually €0.10 cheaper. Fuel is marginally more expensive in Dublin. In Northern Ireland, petrol costs between £1.20 and £1.30 per litre, but diesel is slightly more expensive (between £1.25 and £1.35 per litre).

Service Stations These are ubiquitous on all national roads, usually on the outskirts of towns. They're increasingly harder to find in cities, and the motorway network has only three or four spread across the entire system. In the North, the big supermarket chains have gotten into the fuel business, so you can fill your car before or after you shop. There are service stations along the North's motorway network.

SAFETY

Although driving in Ireland is a relatively pain-free experience, hire cars and cars with foreign registrations can be targeted by thieves looking to clean them of their contents. Don't leave any valuables, including bags and suitcases, on display. Overnight parking is safest in covered car parks.

BORDER CROSSINGS

Border crossings between Northern Ireland and the Republic are unnoticeable; there are no formalities of any kind. This may change, however, once Brexit occurs in 2020

RADIO

The Irish love radio – up to 85% of the population listens in on any given day. Following are the national radio stations:

Newstalk 106-108 (106-108FM) News, current affairs and lifestyle.

RTE Radio 1 (88.2-90FM) Mostly news and discussion.

RTE Radio 2 (90.4-92.2FM) Lifestyle and music.

RTE Lyric FM (96-99FM) Classical music.

Today FM (100-102FM) Music, chat and news.

Regional or local radio is also very popular, with 25 independent local radio stations available, depending on your location.

In Northern Ireland, the BBC rules supreme, with BBC Radio Ulster (92.7-95.4FM) flying the local flag in addition to the four main BBC stations.

Local Expert: Driving Tips

Conor Faughnan, Director of Consumer Affairs with the Automobile Association, shares his tips for hassle-free driving in Ireland:

➡ The motorway network is excellent, but there aren't nearly enough rest areas so check that you have a full tank of fuel before setting off. Off the motorway network there is a good supply of service stations, often open 24 hours, but less so in more remote areas.

➡ The real driving fun is on Ireland's network of secondary roads, where road conditions vary – make sure you're equipped with a good map along with your sat-nav, and beware of potholes, poor road surfaces and corners obscured by protruding hedges! You may also encounter farm machinery and even livestock on rural roads.

➡ Although it rarely snows, winter conditions can be testing (particularly when roads are icy).

➡ A driver may flash their hazard lights once or twice as an informal way to say 'thank you' for any kind of road courtesy extended to them.

Driving Problem-Buster

What should I do if my car breaks down? Call the service number of your car-hire company and a local garage will be contacted. If you're bringing your own car, it's a good idea to join the Automobile Association Ireland, which covers the whole country, or, in Northern Ireland, the Royal Automobile Club (RAC), which can be called to attend breakdowns at any time.

What if I have an accident? Hire cars usually have a leaflet in the glovebox about what to do in case of an accident. Exchange basic information with the other party (name, insurance details, driver's licence number, company details if the car's a rental). No discussion of liability needs to take place at the scene. It's a good idea to photograph the scene of the accident, noting key details (damage sustained, car positions on the road, any skid markings). Call the police (☑999) if required.

What should I do if I get stopped by police? Always remain calm and polite: police are generally courteous and helpful. They will want to see your passport (or valid form of ID), licence and proof of insurance. In the Republic, breath testing is mandatory if asked.

What if I can't find anywhere to stay? If you're travelling during the summer months, always book your accommodation in advance. If you're stuck, call the local tourist office's accommodation hotline.

How do I pay for tollways? Tolls are paid by putting cash in the bucket as you pass. If you don't have exact change, at least one booth is staffed.

Ireland Travel Guide

GETTING THERE & AWAY

AIR

Ireland's main airports:

Cork Airport (☎021-431 3131; www.corkairport.com) Airlines servicing the airport include Aer Lingus and Ryanair.

Dublin Airport (☎01-814 1111; www.dublinairport.com) Ireland's major international gateway airport, with direct flights from the UK, Europe, North America and the Middle East.

Shannon Airport (SNN; ☎061-712 000; www.shannonairport.ie; ☎) Has a few direct flights from the UK, Europe and North America.

Northern Ireland's airports:

Belfast International Airport (Aldergrove; ☎028-9448 4848; www.belfastairport.com; Airport Rd) Has direct flights from the UK, Europe and North America.

Car hire firms are well represented at all major airports. Regional airports will have at least one internationally recognised firm as well as local operators.

Book Your Stay Online

For more accommodation reviews by Lonely Planet authors, check out http://hotels.lonelyplanet.com. You'll find independent reviews, as well as recommendations on the best places to stay. Best of all, you can book online.

SEA

The main ferry routes between Ireland and the UK and mainland Europe:

➡ Belfast to Liverpool (England; eight hours)
➡ Belfast to Cairnryan (Scotland; 1¾ hours)
➡ Cork to Roscoff (France; 14 hours; April to October only)
➡ Dublin to Liverpool (England; fast/slow four/8½ hours)
➡ Dublin & Dun Laoghaire to Holyhead (Wales; fast/slow two hours/3½ hours)
➡ Larne to Cairnryan (Scotland; two hours)
➡ Larne to Troon (Scotland; two hours; March to October only)
➡ Larne to Fleetwood (England; six hours)
➡ Rosslare to Cherbourg/Roscoff (France; 18/20½ hours)
➡ Rosslare to Fishguard & Pembroke (Wales; 3½ hours)

Competition from budget airlines has forced ferry operators to discount heavily and offer flexible fares. A useful website is www.ferrybooker.com, which covers all sea-ferry routes and operators to Ireland.
Main operators include the following:

Brittany Ferries (www.brittanyferries.com) Cork to Roscoff; April to October.

Irish Ferries (www.irishferries.com) It has Dublin to Holyhead ferries (up to four per day year-round) and France to Rosslare (three times per week).

P&O Ferries (www.poferries.com) Daily sailings year-round from Dublin to Liverpool, and Larne to Cairnryan. Larne to Troon runs March to October only.

Stena Line (www.stenaline.com) Daily sailings from Holyhead to Dublin Port, from Belfast to Liverpool and Cairnryan, and from Rosslare to Fishguard.

Arriving in Ireland

Dublin Airport Private coaches run every 10 to 15 minutes to the city centre (€6). Taxis take 30 to 45 minutes and cost €20 to €30.

Dun Laoghaire Ferry Port Public bus takes around 45 minutes to the centre of Dublin; DART (suburban rail) takes about 25 minutes. Both cost €3.

Dublin Port Terminal Buses are timed to coincide with arrivals and departures; they cost €3.50 to the city centre.

Belfast International Airport Airport Express 300 bus runs hourly (one way/return £8/11.50, 30 to 55 minutes). A taxi costs around £30.

George Best Belfast City Airport Airport Express 600 bus runs every 20 minutes (one way/return £2.60/4, 15 minutes). A taxi costs around £10.

IRELAND TRAVEL GUIDE ACCOMMODATION

DIRECTORY A–Z

ACCOMMODATION

Accommodation options range from bare and basic to pricey and palatial. The spine of the Irish hospitality business is the ubiquitous B&B, in recent years challenged by a plethora of midrange hotels and guesthouses. Beyond Expedia, Booking.com, Trivago and other hotel price comparison sites, Ireland-specific online resources for accommodation include the following:

Daft.ie (www.daft.ie) Online property portal includes holiday homes and short-term rentals.

Elegant Ireland (www.elegant.ie) Specialises in self-catering castles, period houses and unique properties.

Imagine Ireland (www.imagineireland.com) Holiday cottage rentals throughout the whole island, including Northern Ireland.

Irish Landmark Trust (www.irishlandmark.com) Not-for-profit conservation group that rents self-catering properties of historical and cultural significance, such as castles, tower houses, gate lodges, schoolhouses and lighthouses.

Lonely Planet (www.lonelyplanet.com/Ireland/hotels) Recommendations and bookings.

Dream Ireland (www.dreamireland.com) Lists self-catering holiday cottages and apartments.

B&Bs & Guesthouses

Bed and breakfasts are small, family-run houses, farmhouses and period country houses, generally with fewer than five bedrooms. Standards vary enormously, but most have some bedrooms with private bathroom at a cost of roughly €40 to €60 (£35 to £50) per person per night (at least €100 in Dublin). In luxurious B&Bs, expect to pay €70 (£60) or more per person. Off-season rates – usually October through to March – are usually lower, as are midweek prices.

Guesthouses are like upmarket B&Bs, but a bit bigger. Facilities are usually better and sometimes include a restaurant.

Other tips:

➡ Facilities in B&Bs range from basic (bed, bathroom, kettle, TV) to beatific (whirlpool baths, rainforest showers) as you go up in price. Wi-fi is standard and most have parking (but check).

➡ Most B&Bs take credit cards, but the occasional rural one might not; check when you book.

➡ Advance reservations are strongly recommended, especially in peak season (June to September).

➡ Some B&Bs and guesthouses in more remote regions may only be open from Easter to September or other months.

➡ If full, B&B owners may recommend another house in the area (possibly a private house taking occasional guests, not in tourist listings).

➡ To make prices more competitive at some B&Bs, breakfast may be optional.

Camping & Caravan Parks

Camping and caravan parks aren't as common in Ireland as they are elsewhere in Europe. Some hostels have camping space for tents and also offer house facilities, which makes them better value than the main camping grounds.

At commercial parks the cost is typically somewhere between €15 and €25 (£12 to £20) for a tent and two people. Prices given for campsites are for two people unless stated otherwise. Caravan sites cost around €20 to €30 (£17 to £25). Most parks are open only from Easter to the end of September or October.

Hostels

Prices quoted for hostel accommodation apply to those aged over 18. A high-season dorm bed generally costs €12 to €25, or €18 to €30 in Dublin (£15 to £20 in Northern Ireland). Many hostels now have family and double rooms.

Relevant hostel associations:

An Óige (www.anoige.ie) HI-associated national organisation with 26 hostels scattered around the Republic.

HINI (www.hini.org.uk) HI-associated organisation with five hostels in Northern Ireland.

Independent Holiday Hostels of Ireland (www.hostels-ireland.com) Fifty-five tourist-board-approved hostels throughout all of Ireland.

Independent Hostel Owners of Ireland (www.independenthostelsireland.com) Independent hostelling association.

ELECTRICITY

220V/50Hz

FOOD

The 'local food' movement was pioneered in Ireland in the 1970s, notably at the world-famous Ballymaloe House. Since then the movement has gone from strength to strength, with dozens of farmers markets showcasing the best of local produce, and restaurants all over the country highlighting locally sourced ingredients.

A 'Standard' Hotel Rate?

There is no such thing. Prices vary according to demand – or have different rates for online, phone or walk-in bookings. B&B rates are more consistent, but virtually every other accommodation will charge wildly different rates depending on the time of year, day, festival schedule and even your ability to do a little negotiating. The following price ranges have been used in our reviews of places to stay. Prices are all based on a double room with private bathroom in high season.

Budget (€)	<€80
Midrange (€€)	€80–180
Top end (€€€)	>€180

When to Eat

Irish eating habits have changed over the last couple of decades, and there are differences between urban and rural practices.

Breakfast Usually eaten before 9am, as most people rush off to work (though hotels and B&Bs will serve until 10am or 11am Monday to Friday, and till noon at weekends in urban areas). Weekend brunch is popular in bigger towns and cities.

Lunch Urban workers eat on the run between 12.30pm and 2pm (most restaurants don't begin to serve lunch until at least midday). At weekends, especially Sunday, the midday lunch is skipped in favour of a substantial mid-afternoon meal (called dinner), usually between 2pm and 4pm.

Tea Not the drink, but the evening meal – also confusingly called dinner. This is the main meal of the day for urbanites, usually eaten around 6.30pm. Rural communities eat at the same time but with a more traditional tea of bread, cold cuts and, yes, tea. Restaurants follow international habits, with most diners not eating until at least 7.30pm.

Supper A before-bed snack of tea and toast or sandwiches, still enjoyed by many Irish folk, though urbanites increasingly eschew it for health reasons. Not a practice in restaurants.

Vegetarians & Vegans

Ireland has come a long, long way since the days when vegetarians were looked upon as odd creatures; nowadays, even the most militant vegan will barely cause a ruffle in all but the most basic of kitchens. Which isn't to say that travellers with plant-based diets are going to find the most imaginative range of options on menus outside the bigger towns and cities – or in the plethora of modern restaurants that have opened in the last few years – but you can rest assured that the overall quality of the homegrown vegetable is top-notch and most places will have at least one dish that you can tuck into comfortably.

LGBTQI+ TRAVELLERS

Ireland is a generally tolerant place for the LGBTQI+ community. Bigger cities such as Dublin, Galway and Cork have well-

Eating Price Ranges

The folllowing price indicators, used throughout this guide, represent the cost of a main dish:

Budget (€)	<€12
Midrange (€€)	€12–25
Top end (€€€)	>€25

established gay scenes, as do Belfast and Derry in Northern Ireland. Same-sex marriage has been legal in the Republic since 2015; Northern Ireland is the only region of the United Kingdom where it is not.

While the cities and main towns tend to be progressive and tolerant, you'll still find pockets of homophobia throughout the island, particularly in smaller towns and rural areas.

Resources include the following:

Gaire (www.gaire.com) Message board and info for a host of gay-related issues.

Gay & Lesbian Youth Northern Ireland (www.cara-friend.org.uk) Voluntary counselling, information, health and social-space organisation for the gay community.

Gay Men's Health Service (☑01 921 2730; www.hse.ie/go/GMHS) Practical advice on men's health issues.

National LGBT Federation (NLGF; ☑01-671 9076; http://nxf.ie) Publishes the monthly *Gay Community News* (www.gcn.ie).

Northern Ireland Gay Rights Association (☑028-9066 5257; www.nidirect.gov.uk; 9-13 Waring St) Represents the rights and interests of the LGBTQI+ community in Northern Ireland. It offers phone and online support, but is not a call-in centre.

Outhouse (☑01-873 4999; www.outhouse.ie; 105 Capel St; ⊙10am-6pm Mon-Fri, noon-5pm Sat; ▣all city centre) Top LGBTQI+ resource centre in Dublin. Great stop-off point to see what's on, check noticeboards, visit the cafe and library, and meet people. The website has listings and support links.

Dining Etiquette

The Irish aren't big on restrictive etiquette, preferring friendly informality to any kind of stuffy to-dos. Still, the following are a few tips to dining with the Irish:

Children All restaurants welcome kids up to 7pm, but pubs and some smarter restaurants don't allow them in the evening. Family restaurants have children's menus; others have reduced portions of regular menu items.

Returning a dish If the food is not to your satisfaction, it's best to politely explain what's wrong with it as soon as you can. Any respectable restaurant will offer to replace the dish immediately.

Paying the bill If you insist on paying the bill for everyone, be prepared for a first, second and even third refusal to countenance such an exorbitant act of generosity. But don't be fooled: the Irish will refuse something several times even if they're delighted with it. Insist gently but firmly and you'll get your way!

HEALTH

No jabs are required to travel to Ireland. Excellent health care is readily available. For minor, self-limiting illnesses, pharmacists can give valuable advice and sell over-the-counter medication. They can also advise when more specialised help is required and point you in the right direction.

EU citizens equipped with a European Health Insurance Card (EHIC), available from health centres or UK post offices, will be covered for most medical care – but not non-emergencies or emergency repatriation. While other countries, such as Australia, also have reciprocal agreements with Ireland and Britain, many do not.

In Northern Ireland, everyone receives free emergency treatment at accident and emergency (A&E) departments of state-run NHS hospitals, irrespective of nationality.

INTERNET ACCESS

Wi-fi and 3G/4G networks are making internet cafes largely redundant (except to gamers). The few that are left will charge around €6 per hour. Most accommodation places have wi-fi, either free or for a daily charge (up to €10 per day).

MONEY

The Republic of Ireland uses the euro (€). Northern Ireland uses the pound sterling (£), though the euro is also accepted in many places. Although notes issued by Northern Irish banks are legal tender

throughout the UK, many businesses outside of Northern Ireland refuse to accept them and you'll have to swap them in British banks.

ATMs

All banks have ATMs that are linked to international money systems such as Cirrus, Maestro or Plus. Each transaction incurs a currency-conversion fee, and credit cards can incur immediate and exorbitant cash-advance interest-rate charges. Watch out for ATMs that have been tampered with, as card-reader scams ('skimming') have become a real problem.

Credit & Debit Cards

Visa and MasterCard credit and debit cards are widely accepted in Ireland. American Express is only accepted by the major chains, and very few places accept Diners or JCB. Smaller businesses, such as pubs and some B&Bs, prefer debit cards (and will charge a fee for credit cards), and a small number of rural B&Bs only take cash.

Exchange Rates

The Republic of Ireland uses the euro.

Australia	A$1	€0.62
Canada	C$1	€0.68
Japan	Y100	€0.83
New Zealand	NZ$1	€0.60
UK	£1	€1.12
USA	US$1	€0.89

OPENING HOURS

Banks 10am–4pm Monday to Friday (to 5pm Thursday)

Pubs 10.30am–11.30pm Monday to Thursday, 10.30am–12.30am Friday and Saturday, noon–11pm Sunday (30 minutes 'drinking up' time allowed); closed Christmas Day and Good Friday

Restaurants noon–10.30pm; many close one day of the week

Shops 9.30am–6pm Monday to Saturday (to 8pm Thursday in cities), noon–6pm Sunday

PHOTOGRAPHY

➡ Natural light can be very dull, so use higher ISO speeds than usual, such as 400 for daylight shots.

➡ In Northern Ireland get permission before taking photos of fortified police stations, army posts or other military or quasi-military paraphernalia.

➡ Don't take photos of people in Protestant or Catholic strongholds of West Belfast without permission; always ask and be prepared to accept a refusal.

➡ Lonely Planet's *Guide to Travel Photography* is full of helpful tips for photography while on the road.

PUBLIC HOLIDAYS

Public holidays can cause road chaos as everyone tries to get somewhere else for the break. It's wise to book accommodation in advance for these times.

The following are public holidays in both the Republic and Northern Ireland:

New Year's Day 1 January
St Patrick's Day 17 March
Easter March/April
May Holiday 1st Monday in May
Christmas Day 25 December
St Stephen's Day
(Boxing Day) 26 December

St Patrick's Day and St Stephen's Day holidays are taken on the following Monday when they fall on a weekend. Nearly everywhere in the Republic closes on Good Friday even though it isn't an official public holiday. In the North most shops open on Good Friday, but close the following Tuesday.

Republic

June Holiday 1st Monday in June
August Holiday 1st Monday in August
October Holiday Last Monday in October

SAFE TRAVEL

Ireland is safer than most countries in Europe, but normal precautions should be observed.

➡ Don't leave anything visible in your car when you park.

➡ Skimming at ATMs is an ongoing problem; be sure to cover the keypad with your hand when you input your PIN.

Practicalities

Smoking Smoking is illegal in all indoor public spaces, including restaurants and pubs.

Time Ireland uses the 12-hour clock and is on Western European Time (UTC/GMT November to March; plus one hour April to October).

TV & DVD All TV in Ireland is digital terrestrial; Ireland is DVD Region 2.

Weights & Measures In the Republic, both imperial and metric units are used for most measures except height, which is in feet and inches only. Distance is measured in kilometres, but people can refer to it colloquially in miles. In the north, it's imperial all the way.

➡ In Northern Ireland exercise extra care in 'interface' areas where sectarian neighbourhoods adjoin.

➡ Best avoid Northern Ireland during the climax of the Orange marching season on 12 July. Sectarian passions are usually inflamed and even many Northerners leave the province at this time.

TAXES & REFUNDS

Non-EU residents can claim Value Added Tax (VAT, a sales tax of 21% added to the purchase price of luxury goods – excluding books, children's clothing and educational items) back on their purchases, so long as the store operates either the Cashback or Taxback refund program (they should display a sticker). You'll get a voucher with your purchase that must be stamped at the *last point of exit* from the EU. If you're travelling on to Britain or mainland Europe from Ireland, hold on to your voucher until you pass through your final customs stop in the EU; it can then be stamped and you can post it back for a refund of duty paid.

VAT in Northern Ireland is 20%; shops participating in the Tax-Free Shopping refund scheme will give you a form or invoice on request to be presented to customs when you leave. After customs have certified the form, it will be returned to the shop for a refund and the cheque sent to you at home.

TELEPHONE

When calling Ireland from abroad, dial your international access code, followed by ☎353 and the area code (dropping the 0). Area codes in the Republic have three digits, eg ☎021 for Cork, ☎091 for Galway and ☎061 for Limerick. The only exception is Dublin, which has a two-digit code (☎01).

To make international calls from Ireland, first dial 00 then the country code, followed by the local area code and number. Always use the area code if calling from a mobile phone, but you don't need it if calling from a fixed-line number within the area code.

In Northern Ireland the area code for all fixed-line numbers is ☎028, but you only need to use it if calling from a mobile phone or from outside Northern Ireland. To call Northern Ireland from the Republic,

use ☎048 instead of ☎028, without the international dialling code.

Country Code	☎353
International Access Code	☎00
Directory Enquiries	☎11811/ ☎11850
International Directory Enquiries	☎11818

Mobile Phones

➡ Ensure your mobile phone is unlocked for use in Ireland.

➡ Pay-as-you-go mobile phone packages with any of the main providers start around €40 and usually include a basic handset and credit of around €10.

➡ SIM-only packages are also available, but make sure your phone is compatible with the local provider.

TOURIST INFORMATION

In both the Republic and the North there's a tourist office or information point in almost every big town. Most can offer a variety of services, including accommodation and attraction reservations, currency-changing services, map and guidebook sales and free publications.

In the Republic the tourism purview falls to **Fáilte Ireland** (☎Republic 1850 230 330, UK 0800 039 7000; www.discoverireland.ie); in Northern Ireland, it's **Discover Northern Ireland** (☎head office 028-9023 1221; www.discovernorthernireland.com). Outside Ireland both organisations unite under the banner Tourism Ireland (www.tourismireland.com).

TRAVELLERS WITH DISABILITIES

All new buildings have wheelchair access, and many hotels (especially urban ones that are part of chains) have installed lifts, ramps and other facilities such as hearing loops. Others, particularly B&Bs, have not invested in making their properties accessible.

In big cities, most buses have low-floor access and priority space on board, but the number of kneeling buses on regional routes is still relatively small.

Trains are accessible with help. In theory, if you call ahead, an employee of Irish Rail (Iarnród Éireann) will arrange to accompany you to the train. Newer trains have audio and visual information systems for visually impaired and hearing-impaired passengers.

The **Citizens' Information Board** (☎0761 079 000; www.citizensinformationboard. ie) in the Republic and **Disability Action** (☎028-9029 7880; www.disabilityaction.org; 189 Airport Rd W, Portside Business Pk; 🖥28) in Northern Ireland can give some advice to travellers with disabilities.

Lonely Planet's free Accessible Travel guide can be downloaded here: http:// lptravel.to/AccessibleTravel.

VISAS

If you're a European Economic Area (EEA) national, you don't need a visa to visit (or work in) either the Republic or Northern Ireland. Citizens of Australia, Canada, New Zealand, South Africa and the US can visit the Republic for up to three months, and Northern Ireland for up to six months. They are not allowed to work, unless sponsored by an employer.

Full visa requirements for visiting the Republic are available online at www.dfa. ie; for Northern Ireland's visa requirements see www.gov.uk/government/ organisations/uk-visas-and-immigration.

To stay longer in the Republic, contact the local *garda* (police) station or the **Garda National Immigration Bureau** (☎01-666 9100; www.garda.ie; 13-14 Burgh Quay, Dublin; ☻8am-9pm Mon-Fri; 🖥all city centre). To stay longer in Northern Ireland, contact the Home Office (www.gov.uk/ government/organisations/uk-visas-and-immigration).

Language

Irish (Gaeilge) is the country's official language. In 2003 the government introduced the Official Languages Act, whereby all official documents and street signs must be either in Irish or in both Irish and English. Despite its official status, Irish is really only spoken in pockets of rural Ireland known as the Gaeltacht, the main ones being Cork (Corcaigh), Donegal (Dún na nGall), Galway (Gaillimh), Kerry (Ciarraí) and Mayo (Maigh Eo).

Ask people outside the Gaeltacht if they can speak Irish and nine out of 10 of them will probably reply, 'ah, cupla focal' (a couple of words), and they generally mean it – but many adults also regret not having a greater grasp of it. Irish is a compulsory subject in both primary and secondary schools. In recent times, a new Irish curriculum has been introduced cutting the hours devoted to the subject but making the lessons more fun, practical and celebratory.

Irish divides vowels into long (those with an accent) and short (those without), and also distinguishes between broad (a, á, o, ó, u) and slender (e, é, i and í), which can affect the pronunciation of preceding consonants. Other than a few clusters, such as mh and bhf (both pronounced as w), consonants are generally pronounced the same as in English.

Irish has three main dialects: Connaught Irish (in Galway and northern Mayo), Munster Irish (in Cork, Kerry and Waterford) and Ulster Irish (in Donegal). Our pronunciation guides are an anglicised version of modern standard Irish, which is essentially an amalgam of the three – if you read them as if they were English, you'll be able to get your point across in Gaeilge without even having to think about the specifics of Irish pronunciation or spelling.

BASICS

Hello.
Dia duit.   deea gwit

Hello. (reply)
Dia is Muire duit.   deeas moyra gwit

Good morning.
Maidin mhaith.   mawjin wah

Good night.
Oíche mhaith.   eekheh wah

Goodbye. (when leaving)
Slán leat.   slawn lyat

Goodbye. (when staying)
Slán agat.   slawn agut

Yes.
Tá.   taw

No.
Níl.   neel

It is.
Sea.   sheh

It isn't.
Ní hea.   nee heh

Thank you (very) much.
Go raibh (míle)   goh rev (meela)
maith agat.   mah agut

Excuse me.
Gabh mo leithscéal.   gamoh lesh scale

I'm sorry.
Tá brón orm.   taw brohn oruhm

Do you speak (Irish)?
An bhfuil (Gaeilge) agat?   on wil (gaylge) oguht

I don't understand.
Ní thuigim.   nee higgim

What is this?
Cad é seo?   kod ay shoh

Want More?

For in-depth language information and handy phrases, check out Lonely Planet's *Irish Language & Culture*. You'll find it at **shop.lonelyplanet.com**, or you can buy Lonely Planet's iPhone phrasebooks at the Apple App Store.

Signs

Dúnta	Closed
Fir	Men
Gardaí	Police
Leithreas	Toilet
Mná	Women
Ná Caitear Tobac	No Smoking
Oifig An Phoist	Post Office
Oifig Eolais	Tourist Information
Oscailte	Open
Páirceáil	Parking

What is that?
Cad é sin? — kod ay shin

I'd like to go to ...
Ba mhaith liom dul go dtí ... — baw wah lohm dull go dee ...

I'd like to buy ...
Ba mhaith liom ... a cheannach. — bah wah lohm ... a kyanukh

another/one more
ceann eile — kyawn ella

nice
go deas — goh dyass

MAKING CONVERSATION

Welcome.
Ceád míle fáilte. — kade meela fawlcha
(lit: 100,000 welcomes)

Bon voyage!
Go n-éirí an bóthar leat! — go nairee on bohhar lat

How are you?
Conas a tá tú? — kunas aw taw too

I'm fine.
Táim go maith. — thawm go mah

... please.
... más é do thoil é. — ... maws ay do hall ay

Cheers!
Slainte! — slawncha

What's your name?
Cad is ainm duit? — kod is anim dwit

My name is (Sean Frayne).
(Sean Frayne) is ainm dom. — (shawn frain) is anim dohm

Impossible!
Ní féidir é! — nee faydir ay

Nonsense!
Ráiméis! — rawmaysh

That's terrible!
Go huafásach! — guh hoofawsokh

Take it easy.
Tóg é gobogé . — tohg ay gobogay

DAYS OF THE WEEK

Monday	*Dé Luaín*	day loon
Tuesday	*Dé Máirt*	day maart
Wednesday	*Dé Ceádaoin*	day kaydeen
Thursday	*Déardaoin*	daredeen
Friday	*Dé hAoine*	day heeneh
Saturday	*Dé Sathairn*	day sahern
Sunday	*Dé Domhnaigh*	day downick

NUMBERS

1	*haon*	hayin
2	*dó*	doe
3	*trí*	tree
4	*ceatháir*	kahirr
5	*cúig*	kooig
6	*sé*	shay
7	*seacht*	shocked
8	*hocht*	hukt
9	*naoi*	nay
10	*deich*	jeh
11	*haon déag*	hayin jague
12	*dó dhéag*	doe yague
20	*fiche*	feekhe
21	*fiche haon*	feekhe hayin

BEHIND THE SCENES

SEND US YOUR FEEDBACK

We love to hear from travellers – your comments help make our books better. We read every word, and we guarantee that your feedback goes straight to the authors. Visit **lonelyplanet. com/contact** to submit your updates and suggestions.

Note: We may edit, reproduce and incorporate your comments in Lonely Planet products such as guidebooks, websites and digital products, so let us know if you don't want your comments reproduced or your name acknowledged. For a copy of our privacy policy visit lonelyplanet.com/privacy.

ACKNOWLEDGMENTS

Climate map data adapted from Peel MC, Finlayson BL & McMahon TA (2007) 'Updated World Map of the Köppen-Geiger Climate Classification', *Hydrology and Earth System Sciences*, 11, 163344.

Cover photographs: Front: Country road in County Sligo, Cahir Davitt/Alamy ©; Back: Cliffs of Moher, Patryk Kosmider/Shutterstock ©

THIS BOOK

This 1st edition of *Galway & the West of Ireland Road Trips* was researched and written by Belinda Dixon. This guidebook was produced by the following:

Destination Editor Cliff Wilkinson

Senior Product Editors Daniel Bolger, Jessica Ryan

Regional Senior Cartographer Mark Griffiths

Cartographer Julie Sheridan

Product Editor Will Allen

Book Designer Katherine Marsh

Assisting Editors Andrew Bain, Imogen Bannister, Nigel Chin, Carly Hall, Kellie Langdon, Lou McGregor, Rosie Nicholson, Kristin Odijk, Gabrielle Stefanos, Simon Williamson

Assisting Cartographer Alison Lyall

Cover Researcher Naomi Parker

Thanks to Sasha Drew, Susan Paterson, Rachel Rawling, Angela Tinson

OUR STORY

A beat-up old car, a few dollars in the pocket and a sense of adventure. In 1972 that's all Tony and Maureen Wheeler needed for the trip of a lifetime – across Europe and Asia overland to Australia. It took several months, and at the end – broke but inspired – they sat at their kitchen table writing and stapling together their first travel guide, *Across Asia on the Cheap*. Within a week they'd sold 1500 copies. Lonely Planet was born.

Today, Lonely Planet has offices in Franklin, London, Melbourne, Oakland, Dublin, Beijing and Delhi, with more than 600 staff and writers. We share Tony's belief that 'a great guidebook should do three things: inform, educate and amuse'.

INDEX

---

000 Map pages

OUR WRITERS

BELINDA DIXON

Only happy when her feet are suitably sandy, Belinda has been (gleefully) travelling, researching and writing for Lonely Planet since 2006. It's seen her navigating mountain passes and soaking in hot-pots in Iceland's Westfjords, marvelling at Stonehenge at sunrise; scrambling up Italian mountain paths; horse riding across Donegal's golden sands; gazing at Verona's frescoes; and fossil hunting on Dorset's Jurassic Coast. Then there's the food and drink: truffled mushroom pasta in Salo; whisky in Aberdeen, Balti in Birmingham, grilled fish in Dartmouth; wine in Bardolino. And all in the name of research. Belinda is also a podcaster and adventure writer and helps lead wilderness expeditions. See her blog posts at https://belindadixon.com.

Published by Lonely Planet Global Ltd
CRN 554153
1st edition – March 2020
ISBN 978 1 78868 649 5
© Lonely Planet 2020   Photographs © as indicated 2020
10 9 8 7 6 5 4 3 2 1
Printed in China

Although the authors and Lonely Planet have taken all reasonable care in preparing this book, we make no warranty about the accuracy or completeness of its content and, to the maximum extent permitted, disclaim all liability arising from its use.

All rights reserved. No part of this publication may be copied, stored in a retrieval system, or transmitted in any form by any means, electronic, mechanical, recording or otherwise, except brief extracts for the purpose of review, and no part of this publication may be sold or hired, without the written permission of the publisher. Lonely Planet and the Lonely Planet logo are trademarks of Lonely Planet and are registered in the US Patent and Trademark Office and in other countries. Lonely Planet does not allow its name or logo to be appropriated by commercial establishments, such as retailers, restaurants or hotels. Please let us know of any misuses: lonelyplanet.com/ip.